# ESTHER

## FOR SUCH A TIME
## AS THIS

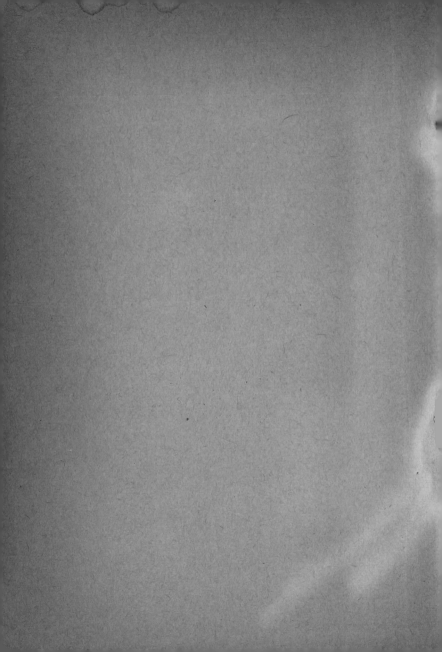

# ESTHER

## FOR SUCH A TIME AS THIS

*by*

CARL ARMERDING

MOODY PRESS

CHICAGO

To my dear sister
Minnie,
faithful and beloved missionary
to
the Indians
of
the great Southwest

# INTRODUCTION

I RAN, universally known among English-speaking people as Persia before March, 1935, and often referred to as such by a good many, is the country in which Esther was born and brought up. The Persians themselves never call their country anything but Iran. It is located in the heart of that part of the world to which we refer as the Middle East. For many years it had little or no political importance, but in recent years its affairs have occupied the headlines of our newspapers again and again.

Many people think of the country only as the source of Persian rugs, so well known both for their quality and their beauty. But it produces other things as well. It is with real sadness of heart that we refer to it as one of the world's largest producers of opium. Its chief source of wealth is its oil. According to reliable geologists "the country fairly floats on oil." But this, as we know, has also been the source of much of its trouble.

Biblically, Persia is also a very important country. In the second chapter of Daniel, often referred to as "the primer of prophecy," we find this country, in association with Media, taking its place as the second great world empire. The Babylonian, of course, was first. Nebuchadnezzar was told by the prophet Daniel that he was "that head of gold." But the capture of the city of Babylon by Cyrus the Persian in the days of Belshazzar marked the end of that empire. It was succeeded by the Medo-Persian Empire, represented in the image or colossus of the second chapter of Daniel, as the breast and arms of silver. In his interpretation of this, Daniel speaks of it as an inferior kingdom (Dan. 2:39). It was inferior in that it was not an absolute monarchy like the Babylonian Empire. It is said of Nebuchadnezzar that "whom he would he slew . . . and whom he would he set up; and whom he would he put down" (Dan. 5:19). Such was evidently not the case with the Persian monarch. Before deposing Vashti, for example, we find that he consults with the nobles (Esther 1:13 ff.).

In Daniel 7:5 this same kingdom is said to be "like to a bear, and it raised up itself on one side, and it had three ribs in the mouth of it between the teeth of it: and they said thus unto it, Arise, devour much flesh." From this we may gather that this empire was both powerful and rapacious. We find this same kingdom mentioned again in Daniel 8:3 where it is described as "a ram which had two horns: and the two horns were high; but one was higher than the other, and the higher came up last." To this the prophet adds, "I saw the ram pushing westward, and northward, and southward; so that no beasts might stand before him, neither was there any that could deliver out of his hand; but he did according to his will, and became great."

Such was the state of the Persian Empire in the days of Esther. We shall see as we proceed with our study that it was enjoying a period of great prosperity. At least there was a show of great prosperity. And doubtless there were many who thought that this would go on indefinitely, little realizing how soon all might be taken from them. From our "primer of prophecy" we know that it was to be overcome by the Greeks just as the Babylonian had been overthrown by the Medes and the Persians. How true it is that "the things which are seen are temporal; but the things which are not seen are eternal" (II Cor. 4:18)!

It has been noticed by all who have made a study of the Book of Esther that the name of God is never mentioned in it. Nevertheless, as we read we are persuaded that "behind the dim unknown, standeth God within the shadow, keeping watch above His own." It has been well said that "no disbeliever in God could have written it; and no believer in God can read it without finding his faith strengthened thereby" (*Pulpit Commentary*). We are not told who actually wrote the book. But the fact that it is anonymous does not make it less authoritative and canonical than those books of the Bible which were autographed. For example, we do not know absolutely, who wrote the Epistle to the Hebrews, but it is generally accepted as a part of the inspired Word of God. And the same is true of other books in the Bible.

The Book of Esther gives us a segment of the history of the Jews which is not supplied elsewhere in the Bible. For instance, it is here that we learn about the origin of the *Feast of Purim* which, as we all know, is celebrated by the Jewish people to this very day. But what concerns the Christian reader even more than these things are the great moral lessons which may be learned from this book. We may be sure that "all these things happened unto them for ensamples: and they are written for our admonition" (I Cor. 10:11). "For whatsoever things were written aforetime were written for our learning, that we through patience and comfort of the scriptures might have hope" (Rom. 15:4). With such words of encouragement before us let us proceed with our study, ever counting upon the blessed Spirit of God to guide us into all truth (John 16:13).

# CONTENTS

# Chapter 1

# IN A PERSIAN PALACE

Now it came to pass in the days of Ahasuerus, (this is Ahasuerus which reigned, from India even unto Ethiopia, over an hundred and seven and twenty provinces)" and generally held to be Xerxes I who reigned in Persia from 485 B.C. until 465 B.C. He should not be confused with the Ahasuerus mentioned in Ezra 4:6 who reigned a good deal earlier than this, nor with the Ahasuerus mentioned in Daniel 9:1 who was the father of Darius, the contemporary of Daniel. It has been suggested that *Ahasuerus* was really more of a title than a personal name. The fact that Ahasuerus is particularly described here as the one who reigned over one hundred and twenty-seven provinces seems to indicate that the writer was aware of others who bore the same name or title. This one is distinguished because of the wide extent of his empire which was great enough to include the Babylonian as one of its provinces.

Xerxes I succeeded his father Darius and was able to regain Egypt, something which his father had been unable to accomplish. But he failed to conquer Greece, even though he exhausted his empire in the attempt to do so. He was assassinated in 465 B.C., and his son Artaxerxes I succeeded him.

From verse 2 of our chapter we learn that he had his

palace in *Shushan* which is indicated as *Susa* on most Bible maps and located 150 miles north of the head of the Persian Gulf. I take it that when it says "when the king Ahasuerus sat on the throne of his kingdom" that that means that he ascended the throne. We have a similar statement in I Chronicles 29:23 concerning King Solomon. "In the third year of his reign," that is, in 483 B.C., "he made a feast unto all his princes and his servants; the power of Persia and Media, the nobles and princes of the provinces, being before him." We are not told exactly how many guests there were. But the number would certainly run into hundreds. And it is quite possible that the list of guests changed from time to time because the feast lasted about six months. Inasmuch as this great gathering took place just previous to Persia's third expedition against Greece (480-479 B.C.), it has been concluded that the real purpose of this gathering was to prepare for that. That seems to be confirmed by the statement that "the power of Persia and Media, the nobles and princes of the provinces" were there. No doubt they came in relays because all could not be absent from their official posts at the same time.

"When he showed the riches of his glorious kingdom, and the honor of his excellent majesty many days, even an hundred and fourscore days"; according to Herodotus it was then that he announced unto them his ambition: "As Cyrus, Cambyses, and Darius, have enlarged the empire, I wish to do the same. I propose to bridge the Hellespont, march through Europe, and fire Athens for burning Sardis and opposing Datis and Artaphernes. By reducing Attica and Greece, the sky will be the only boundary of Persia." The display of all his riches and glory may have been made at this time both to impress them and to inspire them. Others have tried the same since then only to find by sad experience, as he had to learn, that "pride goeth before destruction, and a haughty spirit before a fall" (Prov. 16:18).

"And when these days were expired, the king made a feast unto all the people that were present in Shushan the palace, both unto great and small, seven days, in the court of the garden of the king's palace." This second feast lasted only a week and seems to have been made especially for the people living in the palace. The palace itself was distinct from the city. (See Esther 9:12, 13.) Just how many people lived in the palace we are not told, only that they were "great and small." It would seem from verse 9 of our chapter that only men were present, however.

The description given of the court of the garden in verse 6 shows what a grand place it must have been with its awnings of various colors, "fastened with cords of fine linen and purple to silver rings and pillars of marble." After the manner of the Orient, the guests would recline at the table as they did when our blessed Lord was here on earth. And the beds, or couches, on which they reclined were of gold and silver. This may mean that the coverings were made of cloth of gold and silver, or it may mean that the very beds themselves were actually made of the precious metals. But where we might expect to find expensive Persian rugs there was "a pavement of red, and blue, and white, and black, and marble." According to another translation, these last two were really "alabaster and black marble," or "mother of pearl."

Evidently the main feature of this feast was the drinking of royal wine of which there was an abundance, "according to the state of the king." The cups from which the guests drank were all of gold, but no two alike. The only thing which relieves this sad picture is the statement that the drinking was without constraint, "none did compel." The reason here given for this royal commandment is "that they should do according to every man's pleasure." What that "pleasure" meant we may learn from what follows.

The ninth verse of the chapter lets us know what was going on elsewhere in the palace. Here we learn of another feast given by the queen "for the women in the royal house which belonged to king Ahasuerus." It has been suggested that *Vashti* was not the actual name of the queen but an epithet something like "sweetheart" or "darling." If that be so, it would indicate that she was really a great favorite of the king. Nevertheless, she had a mind of her own and for that we must admire her.

"On the seventh day," just as the feast to all the people was drawing to a close, "when the heart of the king was merry with wine . . . he commanded the seven chamberlains that served" in his presence to bring the queen before him "with the crown royal to show the people and the princes her beauty: for she was fair to look upon." Inasmuch as it was the custom then for women to be heavily veiled, it would be necessary for her to appear unveiled in order for the king to show her beauty to the men assembled there at that time. This evidently was too much for her. To break with that tradition, however trivial it may seem to us now, was too serious a matter to her. Moreover, she probably knew that the king was not the only one whose heart was merry with wine by that time. To have appeared in such company unveiled would have exposed her to possible insult and disgrace. And so she "refused to come at the king's commandment by his chamberlains" or eunuchs.

And now the one who shortly before was merry with wine is "very wroth, and his anger burned in him." How quick is the change from the one extreme to the other when a man has lost all sense of the consideration which is due one who occupies the position of queen of the realm! Nevertheless, he seems to have had sense enough to consult with his "wise men" before taking any action against the queen. We note that these wise men were men "which knew the times." They also "knew law and judgment." Because of this they enjoyed a place of special nearness to the king, they "saw the king's face," and they also "sat the first in the kingdom." Officially, they were "the seven princes of Persia and Media." In our country I suppose that we would call them members of the Cabinet. In Great Britain they would be known as the Privy Council.

The fact that these men "knew the times" may mean that they knew the trend of things. It is possible that Vashti's refusal to obey the command of Ahasuerus was a symptom more than anything else. It is interesting to observe that the king raised the question: "What shall we do unto the queen Vashti according to the law, because she hath not performed the commandment of king Ahasuerus by the chamberlains?" Since they were men who had knowledge of the times as well as of the law, it looks as though they saw in her refusal that which was going to have far-reaching effects. That this is so seems to be clear from the statement made by Memucan when he said before the king and the princes, "Vashti the queen hath not done wrong to the king only, but also to all the princes, and to all the people that are in all the provinces of the king Ahasuerus." But, it should be noted, that there is not even a hint here that she had broken any law which was in force at that time.

There are those who have seen in this a parallel to what Eve did in the Garden of Eden in that her sin also had far-reaching effects. But tempting as it may be for some to indulge in such typological speculation, we must be careful not to read into this simple story what is not there. It seems that these men were afraid that when the news got around that "the king Ahasuerus commanded Vashti the queen to be brought in before him, but she came not," that all the women in the realm would despise their husbands. From verse 18 we learn that they especially feared what might happen in the court itself among "the ladies of Persia and Media." It does seem singular that Vashti's refusal should have such far-reaching effects. It all makes us suspect that some sort of social upheaval was in the making. And that is why it was suggested that Vashti's behavior at this time was a symptom rather than a cause.

The fact that the wise men feared that there would arise "too much contempt and wrath" does look as though there was contempt and wrath already—contempt on the part of the women, and wrath on the part of the men. Thus, in a rather incidental way we get a hint of some of the stresses and strains which there may have been in the social order of that day. And so "the wise men which knew the times" hastened to take steps to prevent, if possible, an upheaval which would have humbled every male in the Persian Empire.

Accordingly we read that they proposed to the king that a royal commandment should go out from him, and that it should become a part of the unalterable laws of the Persians and the Medes, "That Vashti come no more before king Ahasuerus." This was probably tantamount to imprisonment for life. Even though these wise men had the reputation of knowing "law and judgment," they did not act according to either on this occasion. All of which shows that even those who have the reputation for wisdom do not always live up to that reputation. Then, too, we may see in this incident an evidence that the government of Persia was not the same as the absolute rule which had obtained in the days of the Babylonians, inasmuch as this was proposed, not by the king, but by his advisers.

In their advice to the king these "wise men" really gave him more than he had asked for. They not only suggested what should be done to Vashti but they also wanted him to "give her royal estate unto another that is better than she." And the purpose of all this is clearly indicated in verse 20. "When the king's decree which he shall make shall be published throughout all his empire, (for it is great,) all the wives shall give to their husbands honor, both to great and small." While it is true that the official position of Vashti made her offense more serious than if she had been an ordinary housewife, it does look as though there was also the grave possibility that her action would touch off a revolt among the women of that day.

"And the saying pleased the king and the princes; and the king did according to the word of Memucan." Apparently it was just what he wanted to hear or, shall we say, what *they* wanted to hear because the princes are here again associated with him. And "he sent letters into all the king's provinces, into every province according to the writing thereof, and to every people after their language, that every man should bear rule in his own house, and that it should be published according to the language of every people." Just how much work this involved we cannot say exactly. But when we take into account that there were 127 provinces in the empire, we may get some idea of the magnitude of this task. No doubt the decree had to be translated into a number of different languages. It had to be according to the writing, or script, of each province.

The last part of this royal decree has been interpreted to mean "that every man should speak his own language in his family, and not that of his wife, if that were different. This is the plain meaning of the existing text, which cannot bear either of the senses suggested in the Authorised Version" (*Pulpit Commentary*). The American Standard Version merely says "that every man should bear rule in his own house, and should speak according to the language of his people." The new Revised Standard Version is substantially the same. All I can suggest by way of comment is that they did not want to have any change in the customs of the country.

There is one thing which we must not overlook in our study of this matter and that is the fact that in all of this Vashti was never called on to defend herself. Nor does anyone rise up to defend her. Her case is disposed of without the right of being heard in the presence of her accusers. We who have lived in a democracy all of our lives can hardly conceive of such a thing. And yet, I dare say, that there is many a woman living in our country today who has been dealt with in very much the same way. Like Vashti she has had to suffer in silence even though she might have won a legal battle if she had taken the matter to court. Surely, we may learn a very practical lesson from this. And we may apply it to all who may be suffering in like manner today. With true queenly grace Vashti did not allow herself to be drawn into this sad affair which had been magnified out of all proportion by those who seem to have been determined to get rid of her.

Whether or not there was any remorse on the part of Ahasuerus later, we do not know. The opening verse of the next chapter might indicate that. But more than that we cannot say. We do know that "he remembered Vashti" but now the task before his servants is to find one "better than she." Who that may be we are not told as yet. "Man proposes, but God disposes." And even though He is not mentioned in this book, it is not hard to see that He is standing in the shadow "keeping watch above His own."

As for Vashti it is possible that she learned, as another had learned long before her time, that "better is a dry morsel, and quietness therewith, than an house full of sacrifices with strife" (Prov. 17:1).

## Chapter 2

# THE QUEST FOR A QUEEN

IN THE STUDY and interpretation of history there is often room for great diversity of opinion. What seems to be most important to one may appear quite trivial to another. And what seems to be right to one may seem all wrong to another. The chapter now before us may serve as a good illustration of this. Did Esther do wrong in hiding her identity, or was she justified in so doing? Was Mordecai at fault when he charged his cousin not to show "her people nor her kindred"? Some would answer these questions in the affirmative and some in the negative. The best we can do under the circumstances is to carefully study the facts as here presented and seek by God's help to understand them aright.

It is held by some that there is an interval of no great length between chapters 1 and 2 of our book. Nevertheless, it would take some time to send letters to all of the king's provinces inasmuch as means of communication was much slower then than they are now. And that would give ample time for the king to think things over. We read that "the wrath of king Ahasuerus was appeased." The original word for *appeased* is an interesting one. It is the same word which is translated *assuaged* in Genesis 8:1 where it has reference to the subsiding of the waters of the Flood in the days of Noah. We find it again in Esther

7:10 where it is rendered *pacified*. We know that he had been "very wroth, and his anger burned in him" (Esther 1:12). Now that he is sober again, and has had time to reflect on what had been done "he remembered Vashti, and what she had done, and what was decreed against her." More than one commentator has detected here a note of remorse. And one can well see how that might have been the case. Had he been left to himself, he might even have reinstated Vashti. But those who surrounded him would not allow that to happen. The laws of the Medes and Persians may not be changed.

Dr. Ira M. Price in *The Dramatic Story of Old Testament History* takes the view that there was an interval of four years between chapters 1 and 2 of our book, during which "Xerxes was actively engaged in the tremendous overland and sea expeditions against the hated Greeks, who had burned Sardis and otherwise defied the power of Persia. After the disastrous outcome of the entire enterprise at Platea, in 479 B.C., the defeated monarch returned to his capital, humiliated and dishonoured in the eyes of his realm."

"Then said the king's servants that ministered unto him, Let there be fair young virgins sought for the king." It was in this way that they would implement the suggestion they had made that Vashti's royal estate should be given to another, better than she. We note that nothing is said about the social or political qualifications of the prospective queen. Neither is there any reference here to the education or training she should have for the high office she was to hold. Apparently the only qualifications necessary were physical. She must be a fair, young virgin. In this respect the whole proposition differs little from the way in which a movie star might be chosen in our day and time. It is a matter of common knowledge that

Hollywood is constantly in search of "fresh faces." It appears that even when they discover them, they soon lose their freshness after they have been cast in their second or third film. And so the quest continues.

The search for a new queen for the Persians extended to the remotest corners of the empire. Elaborate machinery was set up so that no possible candidate would be overlooked. The ministers of Ahasuerus suggested that "the king appoint officers in all the provinces of his kingdom, that they may gather together all the fair young virgins unto Shushan the palace, to the house of the women, unto the custody of Hege the king's chamberlain, keeper of the women" and that their things for purification be given to them. "And let the maiden which pleaseth the king be queen instead of Vashti." Evidently this met with the royal approval because we read that "the thing pleased the king; and he did so."

By "the house of the women" we are to understand what we would call a harem, that part of an oriental palace or house reserved for the residence of women. King Solomon must have had something like this to accommodate his many wives and concubines. Such an institution naturally accompanies polygamy. "Hege the king's chamberlain" who was in charge was probably some eunuch, perhaps the chief eunuch. He "was usually a repulsive old man, on whom the court ladies are very dependent, and whose favour they are always desirous to secure" (*Jamieson, Fausset and Brown*). The fact that things were given them for "purification" indicates that the king must have been considered almost divine. "It would have been well if the divinity had been himself less impure" (*Pulpit Commentary*). But like a good many today they had double standards, one for the king and another for the people. And there is still many a man who demands utmost purity in the girl he expects to marry, but who has no thought of offering her as much as he expects.

In contrast to all of the above we now have introduced one who is to have a very important place in this whole story. "In Shushan the palace there was a certain Jew, whose name was Mordecai, the son of Jair, the son of Shimei, the son of Kish, a Benjamite." We note that his genealogy was well kept even though he was there in exile. He "had been carried away from Jerusalem with the captivity which had been carried away with Jeconiah king of Judah, whom Nebuchadnezzar the king of Babylon had carried away."

According to II Chronicles 36 there were three different deportations of Jews from Jerusalem in the days of Nebuchadnezzar. The first came in the days of Jehoiakim; the second, in the days of his son Jehoiachin; and the third, in the days of Zedekiah. No doubt the *Jeconiah* referred to here is the same as *Jehoiachin,* who was carried away captive in 597 B.C. If Mordecai was among those carried away at that time, he would now be a very old man. Therefore, it has been thought that the first part of verse 6 refers to his ancestor, Kish. Grammatically, the pronoun *who* might refer to either one. For our present purpose it is not of sufficient importance to go into great detail in connection with it. Some commentators take one view, and some the other. It is sufficient for us to know that he was a descendant of Benjamin and thus a member of the tribe from which the first king of Israel was taken.

Evidently Mordecai was a kindly man for "he brought up Hadassah, that is, Esther, his uncle's daughter: for she had neither father nor mother, and the maid was fair and beautiful; whom Mordecai, when her father and

mother were dead, took for his own daughter." This is
indeed a lovely touch in a chapter which leaves the impression that women were considered just so many ob-
jects which might be shoved around to suit their masters.
Mordecai, being a Jew, would know that the law of
Moses says, "Ye shall not afflict any widow, or fatherless
child" (Exod. 22:22). But he was a man who did more
than the law required. His obedience to it was not merely
negative, it was positive. It is no wonder then that some
commentators have considered him as a type of our Lord
Jesus Christ. Here at any rate he acted according to the
manner of the Lord who "relieveth the fatherless and the
widow" (Ps. 146:9).

The fact that Esther had two names reminds us of
Daniel and his companions. It may be that she got the
name *Esther* in the same way that they got the names
by which they were to be known in the court of Nebuchadnezzar. Her parents had given her the name *Hadassah,* the meaning of which is *myrtle.* The name *Esther*
was probably derived from *Ishtar,* the chief goddess of
the Babylonians and Assyrians. This name was probably
given to her after she was introduced into the harem
of King Ahasuerus. It is not difficult to trace a connection
between *Ishtar* and *star.* According to good authority,
*Ishtar* was the Persian name for the star Venus. If it was
Hege who gave her this name, it may be that she had won
his favor from the very beginning, and that this name
was to be prophetic of her success in the contest for
the queenship.

"So it came to pass, when the king's commandment and
his decree was heard, and when many maidens were
gathered together unto Shushan the palace, to the custody
of Hegai, that Esther was brought also unto the king's
house, to the custody of Hegai, keeper of the women."

From this verse it is clearly seen that this was no mere beauty contest. These virgins were not invited to compete with each other for some coveted prize. While it is true that in a modern beauty contest only one can win, nevertheless, those who do not win are still free to go their own way. Such was not the case here. And one can readily see that no woman would care to go into seclusion for the rest of her life simply because she did not please a capricious man. And in view of this we can also understand why some of the older Jewish commentators and interpreters thought that Mordecai had actually tried to keep his cousin out of all this. But he really had no choice in the matter. It was "the king's commandment and his decree," hardly to be compared with that of a modern constitutional monarch when he requests a command performance.

It is generally held that the *Hegai* who was in charge of these women is the same as the *Hege* of verse 3. And we are told that "the maiden pleased him, and she obtained kindness of him," that is, he favored her. Evidently she made a very favorable impression at once. And it is right here that we begin to see the hand of Him who is not even mentioned by name in this book. But for all that she was favorably received, she had to go through the required procedure for purification. And Hegai "speedily gave her her things for purification, with such things as belonged to her," or, "her portions," according to another version. These portions probably included her food and other necessities. In other words, from now on she would be supported by the king which would be little enough in comparison with all that she had to sacrifice. The "seven maidens, which were meet to be given her, out of the king's house," were appointed to attend her in rotation, one for every day of the week.

As a mark of the high esteem in which Hegai held Esther, "he preferred her and her maids unto the best place of the house of the women." According to the A.S.V. "he removed her," which seems to imply that when she first came into the king's house she had been assigned to a place that was not too nice. In this we may see further evidence of the providence of God. And we have reason to believe that He still works in behalf of His own in similar fashion in our day and time. While much is made of the ill treatment which many of the children of God receive at the hands of the world, we must not overlook the fact that there are also many favors shown us which we cannot account for except that God has been working in our behalf.

Meanwhile "Esther had not showed her people nor her kindred: for Mordecai had charged her that she should not show it." Perhaps if we knew all the circumstances we might understand this better. It is quite possible, of course, that the primary purpose in thus hiding her identity was to protect her from violence. We may be sure that she was not "preferred . . . to the best place of the house of the women" without provoking some to jealousy. And we all know that jealousy can be as cruel as the grave. But in due time she will have to reveal who she is. Of that we have had some examples in our own day. Before the rise of Hitler in Germany there were many Jews who had become so completely identified with the German people that they were no longer referred to as Jews but as Germans. But He who had distinguished His "ancient people" from all other peoples would not allow that to go on. And so we can see the hand of God even in the machinations of a man like Adolf Hitler. No doubt there were Jews in Germany who hid their identity because of personal advantage. But we must not on that account impugn the motives of Mordecai in charging his cousin not to show "her people nor her kindred." We like to believe that he was seeking to shield her from all unnecessary hatred and violence in a time that was not free of anti-Semitism, as we shall see later in our studies.

Since there are those who still question the ethics of all this, it should be pointed out that it is not unethical to withhold information, the revealing of which would serve no good purpose. The fact that Esther did not make known her people nor her kindred certainly did not cause others to suffer. And if, as we have suggested, Mordecai did not want his cousin to get involved in all of this in the first place, then we can see that it was fear rather than ambition which prompted him to charge his cousin as he did.

That he was not completely at ease even after she had been shown favor in the royal harem is indicated in that he "walked every day before the court of the women's house, to know how Esther did, and what should become of her." Because of this it has been thought that he was one of the porters whose business it was to watch the entrance to the palace. It is almost necessary to suppose something like this otherwise it would be difficult to explain his presence there at that time.

To those of us who are accustomed to the modern way of doing things in a hurry what we have here may seem like a waste of time. According to verse 12 of this chapter it took one whole year to prepare these women for their presentation to the king. As we have noticed before, nothing is said about any intellectual or spiritual preparation. That seems not to have been important. The phrase "according to the manner of the women" should read, "according to the law for the women." According to one commentator, this means that which "was probably required by state etiquette." On the other hand, it is quite likely that some of the "fair young virgins" gathered there at that time had come from homes that were none too clean or sanitary. Hence, one can see the necessity for a long season of purification before they might be introduced to his majesty.

We note that these purifications were accomplished first of all "with oil of myrrh" for six months. Myrrh served a double purpose in that it was not only fragrant, it was also credited with having purifying powers as well. It was an ingredient in the holy anointing oil used in the anointing of the priests in Israel. (See Exod. 30:22-33.) It was among the gifts presented by the Magi when they came from the East to worship our Lord Jesus soon after His birth. (See Matt. 2:11.) It was mingled with the wine which was offered to Him when He was suffering upon the cross, "but he received it not" (Mark 15:23). And finally, it was used at His burial when Nicodemus "brought a mixture of myrrh and aloes, about an hundred pound weight" (John 19:39).

From this it will be seen that myrrh had a variety of uses. But the myrrh that is mentioned here is different from that which is mentioned in Genesis 37:25 and 43:11, where a different word is used in the original. The word used here in the Book of Esther means "distilling in drops" suggestive of tears. And while it is not to be supposed that the Persians saw any spiritual significance in this, it is not difficult for the child of God to see that purification before God may be, and usually is, accompanied by tears. But when He who "by himself purged our sins" comes forth in His royal robes, we are told that all of His garments smell of myrrh and aloes and cassia (Ps. 45:8). And it may be that the Persian custom of purification

had its beginnings in that which was originally a divine
institution. In any case such a supposition is not unreasonable because the instructions given to Moses in
Exodus 30 antedated this chapter by a thousand years.

In addition to the myrrh there were "sweet odors . . .
with other things for the purifying of the women." Since
nothing is said about the composition of these things, we
cannot comment on them. It appears that the women
were permitted to request whatever else they might think
necessary over and above that which had been prescribed
by law. Knowing something of the sensuality and lust
of such men as Xerxes, it is possible that some of these
virgins would provide themselves with an aphrodisiac
to arouse his passions even more. So much was at stake.
If a virgin failed to delight him, "she came in unto the
king no more." Small reward indeed for a whole year of
preparation!

How different the case of one who has prepared himself for the service of the King of kings! He, too, may be
privileged to spend but a short time "on the field." But
we may be sure that he will not be cast off on that account. Nay, rather, he will find that the King will delight
in him, and he will yet be "called by name" to enter into
the joy of his Lord.

When Esther's turn came "to go in unto the king, she
required nothing but what Hegai the king's chamberlain,
the keeper of the women appointed." We are not told how
her turn was determined. It may be that they cast lots
for that. But whether or not, she required no extras to
make her more desirable to the man whom she probably
had not even seen until then. If she was at all anxious
about the outcome, we are not told about it here. "And
Esther obtained favor in the sight of all them that looked
upon her." Since it was not the custom for women to

appear in the presence of men unveiled, we conclude that those who looked upon her were women, probably her companions in the "house of the women," and the eunuch who was in charge of them.

"So Esther was taken unto king Ahasuerus into his house royal in the tenth month, which is the month Tebeth, in the seventh year of his reign." The tenth month here corresponds to the latter part of December and the earlier part of January of our present calendar. This is the only time that "the month Tebeth" is mentioned in Scripture. But the interesting thing about it is that it is also called "the tenth month," which is the tenth month of the Jewish *sacred* year and the fourth month of their *civil* year. And it may be that here we have another one of those incidental references which show that even though God is not mentioned by name in this book, He is not left without witness. "The tenth month" was dated from the Passover, the great memorial of Israel's redemption from the bondage of Egypt.

"And the king loved Esther above all the women, and she obtained grace and favor in his sight more than all the virgins; so that he set the royal crown upon her head, and made her queen instead of Vashti." And this is the only reference to love that we have in all of this book, and it is here only that we find the combination "grace and favor," two words which are much used elsewhere in the Old Testament to describe God's attitude toward His people. It is truly remarkable to find them here in this story. But we need not be surprised that terms like these should persist even though the One who ever stands ready to bestow His grace and favor on those who draw nigh to Him has become "the unknown God."

What follows here also seems to be after the divine pattern. "Then the king made a great feast unto all his princes and his servants, even Esther's feast; and he made a release to the provinces, and gave gifts, according to the state of the king." In thus sharing his joy with his princes and his servants the king shows a different spirit from that which he manifested when Vashti refused to obey his royal summons. The fact that this is called "Esther's feast" suggests that this may have been her coronation feast. According to Dr. Jamieson, her crown consisted only of a purple fillet streaked with white, having the appearance of a crown of towers, bound around the forehead. And on the basis of the rendering given in the Septuagint, he says that the feast was really a marriage feast. There is no reason why both ideas may not be combined here.

According to the *Pulpit Commentary*, the "release" was an exemption from taxation, or from military service, or from both, for a specified period. It may be of interest to note that the word for *release* is not the same as that used in Deuteronomy 15 in connection with the year of jubilee. However much that we find here may stimulate the divine pattern, it can never quite equal the original. Nevertheless, one can easily see that this, as well as the giving of gifts, may be used as an illustration of what takes place when we are received by divine grace into God's loving favor. It is said of our Lord that "when he ascended up on high, he led captivity captive, and gave gifts unto men" (Eph. 4:8). And all of this is "according to the state of the king." When we apply that to the King of kings, we find that no earthly monarch can compare with Him; and what happened that day in the Persian palace is like the flicker of a candle in the light of the noonday sun. Our Lord has raised us up together, and made us sit together in heavenly places so that in the ages to come He may show the exceeding riches of His grace in

His kindness toward us through Christ Jesus (see Eph. 2:6, 7).

There is a break at this point in our chapter. A second gathering of virgins probably took place some time after the events which we have just been considering. What the purpose of this gathering may have been, we are not told. But the fact that "then Mordecai sat in the king's gate" sounds as though he had been promoted. Besides the ordinary use of the gates of a city as a place of entry, they were also the place where important business was transacted. Of that we have a good illustration in the case of Boaz and the near kinsman when the question respecting Ruth and the inheritance was decided by ten men of the elders of the city who sat there as judges. (See Ruth 4:1, 2.) It looks as though Lot occupied a similar position in the city of Sodom (Gen. 19:1). With such instances before us it would appear as though Mordecai had been promoted to such a place of honor also.

Parenthetically, as it were, we are told that "Esther had not yet showed her kindred nor her people; as Mordecai had charged her: for Esther did the commandment of Mordecai, like as when she was brought up with him." The fact that she was now queen of the empire did not cause her to change her attitude toward the one who had befriended her when she was left an orphan. Very often, as some of us know from experience, such is not the case. Such obedience and such respect have become the exception rather than the rule in these days.

"In those days, while Mordecai sat in the king's gate, two of the king's chamberlains, Bigthan and Teresh, of those which kept the door, were wroth, and sought to lay hand on the king Ahasuerus." This verse seems to confirm the view that Mordecai was now in a position of trust and honor. And that will explain how it was that the

conspiracy against the life of King Ahasuerus was known
to him. The two men named in this verse evidently occupied a position of special trust also. If the *Bigthan* mentioned here is the *Bigtha* mentioned in Esther 1:10, then
he was one who served in the very presence of the king
himself. Together with Teresh he was charged with the
keeping of the door of the king's sleeping apartment.
(See 6:2.) Thus they might quite readily lay hand on the
king and kill him. Just what their grievance was we are
not told.

Some think that they wanted to avenge Vashti, and that
it was she who instigated this plot. But there is nothing
in the sacred record to support that view. There probably
was some other reason for their anger. And it looks as
though they may have confided in a third party who in
turn told it to Mordecai. And then he "told it unto Esther
the queen." She told it to the king "in Mordecai's name."
This last seems to further confirm the view that Mordecai
was now holding a responsible position as he sat in the
gate. Otherwise his name would not have meant very
much to the king.

But judgment was not pronounced on the guilty pair
until "inquisition was made of the matter." And then "it
was found out"; that is, it was found to be true. And
"therefore they were both hanged on a tree." According
to the great historian, Herodotus, this was the punishment usually meted out to rebels and traitors in Persia
in those days. And the historiographers of that day made
a record of it "in the book of the chronicles of the king."
And there the matter rested until a later day. Apparently
nothing more was done for Mordecai at that time. He
may have resented that. That would be perfectly natural.
But his case was in the hands of a higher Judge who saw
in secret and one day rewarded him openly.

*Chapter 3*

# A CRISIS IN THE MAKING

I N OUR STUDY of chapter 1 we suggested that there was reason to believe that a great social upheaval might have occurred if Vashti had not been deposed because she refused to obey the summons of King Ahasuerus. But in this chapter we see the beginnings of a crisis far more serious than that. In Haman we can easily see a prototype of more modern anti-Semites such as Adolf Hitler, Julius Streicher, and others. But Haman is by no means the first of these Jew-baiters. It must not be overlooked that the main reason why Satan has plotted from time to time to exterminate the Jew is because the Seed, which was to bruise his head, was to come through that people. His bloody attempt to frustrate the divine prediction began with the slaughter of Abel at the hands of his brother Cain.

It has been pointed out by others that Pharaoh's attempt to destroy the firstborn of the Israelites was another link in the chain that was to extend all the way to Calvary and beyond. But Pharaoh's reason for ordering the destruction of all boy babies born to Hebrew mothers was that he feared that they might soon outnumber the Egyptians. Therefore, he said to his people, "Behold, the people of the children of Israel are more and mightier than we: come on, let us deal wisely with them; lest they multiply, and it come to pass, that, when there falleth out any war, they join also unto our enemies, and fight against us, and so get them up out of the land" (Exod. 1:9, 10). From this we learn that he really did not wish to exterminate the Israelites, but he wanted to keep down the number of them so that they could be kept under control. Such was not the case with Haman as we shall see.

Haman is described here as "the son of Hammedatha the Agagite." There has been much discussion as to the exact meaning of the name *Agagite*. Most conservative scholars are agreed that it is a title such as *Pharaoh* in the case of the kings of Egypt, and Abimelech in that of the kings of the Philistines. The earliest Biblical reference to Agag is found in the prophecy of Balaam who said of Israel's King that He "shall be higher than Agag, and his kingdom shall be exalted" (Num. 24:7). The very fact that the Messiah is here compared with Agag gives to the latter an importance which is significant. The force of this is seen as one considers the further prophecies of Balaam who had been hired, as we know, by Balak, the king of Moab, to curse Israel. Even though Balak had ordered Balaam to flee when he found that instead of cursing Israel he had blessed them three times, Balaam again took up his parable in which he becomes more specific than before. Previously he had merely spoken of Israel's enemies in a general way. (See Num. 23:24 and 24:8.) But in his final parable he says, "There shall come a Star out of Jacob, and a Scepter shall rise out of Israel, and shall smite the corners of Moab, and destroy all the children of Sheth."

But my main reason for calling special attention to this parable is the fact that when Balaam looked on Amalek he said, "Amalek was the first of the nations; but his latter end shall be that he perish forever" (Num. 24:20).

The reason for this is given us in the words of Samuel when he said to king Saul, "Thus saith the Lord of hosts, I remember that which Amalek did to Israel, how he laid wait for him in the way, when he came up from Egypt. Now go and smite Amalek, and utterly destroy all that they have, and spare them not. . . . And Saul smote the Amalekites . . . and he took Agag the king of the Amalekites alive, and utterly destroyed all the people with the edge of the sword. But Saul and the people spared Agag," for which he was sharply rebuked by the prophet who himself "hewed Agag in pieces before the Lord in Gilgal" (I Sam. 15:2, 3, 7, 8, 9, 33).

But since the prophecies of Balaam have to do with "the latter days" (Num. 24:14) we need not be surprised to find successors to Agag rising up from time to time to frustrate if possible the purpose of God concerning His people Israel. Such we believe to be the case in the chapter now before us. The Persian Empire in Esther's day included the former kingdom of the Amalekites, "the first of the nations." It is entirely possible that Haman may have been the heir to the throne of Amalek and for that reason was known as "the Agagite." Even if this title refers primarily to his father, Hammedatha, he would naturally inherit it from him. And even though he was not actually reigning as king at the time, there is nothing strange about his retaining the title. In much the same way we might refer to the descendants of the Bourbons, the Hapsburgs, and the Hohenzollerns today.

Our purpose in presenting all of the foregoing is to see in it a possible explanation for the promotion of Haman when Ahasuerus "advanced him, and set his seat above all the princes that were with him." The original word for *seat* in this verse is the word commonly rendered *throne* all through the Old Testament. It is so rendered in Esther 1:2 and 5:1. That makes all the more remarkable the promotion of which we read here. But if Haman was "in the royal line" of the Amalekites, "the first of the nations," then we can see a good reason why Ahasuerus would advance him to a place even above the princes that were with him. From Esther 1:14 we have learned that there were "seven princes of Persia and Media, which saw the king's face, and which sat first in the kingdom." But they were made subordinate to Haman who must have been second only to the king himself.

"And all the king's servants, that were in the king's gate, bowed, and reverenced Haman: for the king had so commanded concerning him." Since, as we have already seen, the gates of the city were something more than a place of entry, these men were also men of distinction. They may have been former officers in the kingdoms which the Persians had subdued. Or, they may have been representatives of those kingdoms. In that case they would consider themselves equal to Haman. Hence, the necessity for a royal command to reverence Haman as one who was now superior to them.

But there was one among them who refused to obey the royal command. "Mordecai bowed not, nor did him reverence." Just why he should be an exception now becomes a matter of inquiry on the part of his fellows who sit in the gate with him. They wanted to know why he was transgressing the king's commandment. It looks as though he paid no attention to them at first. But they kept after him. And "it came to pass, when they spoke daily unto him, and he hearkened not unto them, that they told Haman, to see whether Mordecai's matters would stand: for he had told them that he was a Jew." Perhaps they, too, would like to be excused from having to bow down to Haman. But they could not use the same reason.

Mordecai did not refuse to obey the king's command because he differed with his political views, or for any reason like that. His reason for disobedience was not a matter of choice with him. It was God who had made him a Jew. The fact that he had to tell the others that he was a Jew is interesting. He had lived so long in Persia that he must have become like them. But when the test came, he did not hide the fact that he was not a Persian but a Jew. And we must admire him for that. And so, once again we see the hand of God using the commandment of Ahasuerus to compel His servant to reveal his identity even though it might cost him his life.

"And when Haman saw that Mordecai bowed not, nor did him reverence, then was Haman full of wrath." So enraged was he that "he thought scorn to lay hands on Mordecai alone; for they had showed him the people of Mordecai: wherefore Haman sought to destroy all the Jews that were throughout the whole kingdom of Ahasuerus, even the people of Mordecai." Just why the Jews should be referred to here as "the people of Mordecai" is not revealed unless it be that Mordecai was now identified as their representative on that council which sat "in the king's gate." But no matter what our position may be "none of us liveth to himself, and no man dieth to himself" (Rom. 14:7). The Devil hates the Lord's people, not so much because of who they are, but because of what they are. Our Lord Jesus said, "If the world hate you, ye know that it hated me before it hated you. If ye were of the world, the world would love his own: but because ye are not of the world, but I have chosen you out of the world, therefore the world hateth you" (John 15:18, 19). And even though "the people of Mordecai" had sinned against the Lord, He did not cast them away. We like to think that Mordecai appreciated that and therefore refused to pay homage to another who would, if possible, usurp the place of God.

All of this happened "in the first month, that is, the month Nisan." Nisan is the seventh month of the civil year and the first of the ecclesiastical, or sacred, year. It is the same as the month Abib (Exod. 13:4) which the Lord said was to be to them "the beginning of months." It corresponds to our month of April. And it was "in the twelfth year of king Ahasuerus." That means that it was about five years after the coronation of Queen Esther. That event took place "in the seventh year of his reign" (Esther 2:16).

For one full year, "from day to day, and from month to month, to the twelfth month, that is, the month Adar, "they cast Pur, that is, the lot, before Haman." It is very interesting to find that the word *Pur* comes from a primitive root meaning "to crush, to break, and to bring to nought." In order to determine the right day on which to destroy all the Jews, they cast lots. Evidently "the lot" was called "Pur" in those days because they used rough stones or pebbles for this purpose. Perhaps there is some connection between the crushing, or breaking, and the broken pieces used in casting lots. At the same time there may be also a suggestion of the purpose of all this, that is, the crushing of the Jewish people.

Of course, the Jews themselves used the lot as we know from the ritual of the Day of Atonement (Lev. 16). Moreover, we read in Proverbs 16:33 that "the lot is cast into the lap; but the whole disposing thereof is of the Lord." And it is very evident that the whole disposing of this lot was of the Lord. And thus we get another of those incidental touches in this Book of Esther to show us that God is watching over His own.

Having decided on the day of their destruction beforehand, Haman now goes to obtain the royal approval of his bloody scheme. He says not a word about his personal reasons for desiring the destruction of the Jews. He does not even mention Mordecai by name, nor bring any direct charge against him. He begins by saying, "There is a certan people scattered abroad and dispersed among the people in all the provinces of thy kingdom." In this respect they were different from the other nations which the Persians had subdued. It is reasonable to suppose that the other nations were kept within the former boundaries. But the Jew is different. And it is striking to see that Haman uses the very words that James uses when writing to this same people, addressing them as "the twelve tribes scattered abroad." Similarly, the Apostle Peter writes to "the strangers scattered throughout Pontus," etc. They were scattered indeed, but it was God who had scattered them. But when He did, it was like seed that would take root and spring up in most unpromising soil. No weapon that was formed against them could prosper.

But Haman went on to say that "their laws are diverse from all people." And in that he gave unwitting testimony to the distinctiveness of those laws which had been committed to them at Sinai by the hand of Moses. And no matter how far and wide the recipients may be scattered, this distinction abides. It was because that law was divine that it remained intact, even though those who received those "lively oracles" had repeatedly broken and even despised them. But we like to think that there was still a measure of obedience to that law. We believe that we can see some evidence of that in the fact that Mordecai refused to bow down to Haman. It is not unreasonable to suppose that Haman may have had some knowledge of the real reason why Mordecai would not bow down to him. And if Haman was really an Amalekite, then we can see, too, that there would be a natural hatred in the heart of Mordecai for one who represented one of the bitterest enemies of his people.

But Haman goes on to say, "neither keep they the king's laws: therefore it is not for the king's profit to suffer them." For this statement he offers no proof whatever. Had he carefully considered their past history as a nation, he would never have said that it was "not for the king's profit to suffer them." It is those nations which have not suffered, or tolerated them, who have been the losers. But the nations which have favored them have been blessed because of them.

Haman does not allow the king to decide their fate even though he is polite enough to say, "If it please the king." He it is who wants it to "be written that they may be destroyed." And he stands ready to "pay ten thousand talents of silver into the hands of those that have charge of the business, to bring it into the king's treasuries." Inasmuch as the royal treasuries were quite exhausted at this time because of the expensive campaign against the Greeks, this would be welcome news. No doubt it was a deciding factor. A talent of silver, so we are told, was worth about $2,000. Therefore ten thousand talents would be worth about twenty million dollars. That is a lot of money even at present values. But in that day it must have been worth a great deal more than it would be today. Where Haman was to get all of this money, we are not told. But we may get a hint later.

In giving his ring to Haman the king was really handing over that which would enable Haman to give his bloody plan the royal sanction. But the Scripture is careful to notice that the king "gave it unto Haman the son of Hammedatha the Agagite, the Jews' enemy." And we believe that there is real significance in this repeated description of Haman.

In addition to the royal ring we read that the silver was given to him, and the people also, to do with them as he liked. "The silver" here can hardly refer to the silver which Haman had offered to pay to the king, for it had not yet been paid. It probably refers to the silver of the people whom he now had the authority to exterminate. The confiscation of their goods would naturally follow their liquidation. In giving Haman their silver the king was merely being generous with that which was not his. Bankrupt though he was, he had to keep up the appearance of affluence. And his tribe has by no means died out as yet.

No plan for the evangelization of the world was ever carried out with more precision and attention to detail than we have here. "Then were the king's scribes called on the thirteenth day of the first month, and there was written according to all that Haman had commanded unto the king's lieutenants, and to the governors that were over every province, and to the rulers of every people of every province according to the writing thereof, and to every people after their language." The thirteenth day of the first month would be the day before the Passover had to be killed. By using the royal scribes to write out the proclamation, Haman would be spared the personal expense which would be involved in such a gigantic undertaking.

But it may also be that there were a good many scribes around just waiting for something to do. The lieutenants, governors, and rulers mentioned in this verse probably refer to the three grades of officers. The highest of these would be the lieutenants, or satraps, "the official title of the viceroy, who, in behalf of the Persian monarch, exercised the civil and military authority in several small provinces combined in one government" (*Dictionary of the Bible*, by Davis). The governors would be subordinate to these, whereas the rulers were "native authorities—the head men of the conquered peoples, to whom the Persian system allowed a considerable share of power" (*Pulpit Commentary*). Not one province was overlooked. And the decree was translated into the language of each province so that every last man, woman, and child would know what was to be expected. Would to God we could say as much for the good news of the Gospel! All of this was done in the name of the King Ahasuerus, and sealed with his ring, the seal in this case being the equivalent of his personal signature.

From verse 13 we learn something of the contents of this fateful document. "The letters were sent by posts into all the king's provinces, to destroy, to kill, and to cause to perish, all Jews, both young and old, little children and women, in one day, even upon the thirteenth day of the twelfth month, which is the month Adar, and to take the spoil of them for a prey." As we read these words, we are reminded of the wording of a modern legal document. The objectives are stated in every possible way so that there may be no way of escape on the part of any who might dare to contest its meaning. And the "posts" who carried these letters to the different provinces were couriers who traveled on horseback from one station to another, fresh riders and fresh horses being provided as required to cover the longer distances. We may be sure that if they had had all the means of communication which we now have, they would have availed themselves of them. Should we do less to get out the Gospel to every creature?

In verse 14 we come to the publishing of the commandment to all the people. This is the third step in connection with this document. First it was written. Then it was delivered. And finally it was published. It looks as though the enemy had followed the divine pattern of the Gospel itself. And the couriers, "hastened by the king's commandment," lost no time in delivering it. The fact that "the decree was given in Shushan the palace" shows that it came right from headquarters, as we would say. And so confident are "the king and Haman" that their orders will be faithfully carried out that they can sit down with all leisure "to drink."

"But the city Shushan was perplexed." It is generally thought that "the city" was distinct from "the palace." The common people were evidently filled with apprehension. They probably took slight comfort from the fact that only Jews were involved at the time. It might be their turn next. And history has shown that again and again the fate of Gentiles has been bound up with the fate of the Jews. Even if every Jew in the country were destroyed, he who is a murderer from the beginning would soon be looking for fresh victims. He is well named Apollyon, the Destroyer.

*Chapter 4*

# FAITH AND FATE

THERE ARE COMPARATIVELY few people who will take the time to survey the whole state of affairs when they get into trouble. Some lose their heads altogether, while others just try to "muddle through." As one considers the trouble in which Mordecai found himself, one wonders what other course he might have pursued had he anticipated all that resulted from his refusal to bow down to Haman. We gather from his behavior, as described in the first verse of this chapter, that he was quite surprised at the turn which events took, for when he "perceived all that was done, Mordecai rent his clothes, and put on sackcloth with ashes."

According to Revelation 6:12, it appears that sackcloth was black. It was usually made of goats' hair, and garments made of it "probably resembled a sack, with openings made for the neck and arms, and slit down the front . . . and usually worn over other raiment, but sometimes next to the skin" (Davis). According to one authority, such garments were not even removed at night. In those days sackcloth was the customary attire of mourners. But it was also worn at times by prophets, and frequently captives were dressed in sackcloth. Thus we see that it was symbolic of sorrow, humility, and humiliation.

It will be recalled by those who are conversant with

the story of Joseph that when his brother Reuben discovered that he was no longer in the pit into which his
brothers had cast him before they sold him to the Midi-
anites, "he rent his clothes" as a sign of his grief. And
when Jacob received Joseph's coat which had been dipped
in blood to make it appear that some wild beast had de-
voured him, he also "rent his clothes, and put sackcloth
upon his loins, and mourned for his son many days" (Gen.
37:29-34). Likewise the prophet Daniel when he set his
face unto the Lord his God in prayer and supplication he
did it "with fasting, and sackcloth, and ashes" (Dan. 9:3).

It is entirely possible that Mordecai knew what the
saintly Daniel had done and, finding himself in similar
circumstances, he did likewise. But we must not take that
to mean that he was sorry for what he had done. Evidently he still believed that he had done right in refusing
to bow down to Haman. And that seems to confirm the
view that his refusal was based on religious grounds even
though no reference is made to that here. In any case
he made no secret of his grief. We read that he "went out
into the midst of the city, and cried with a loud and bitter
cry." It has been suggested that Esther and Mordecai, as
well as all the other Jews in Persia at that time, could have
avoided this trouble if they had availed themselves of the
opportunity of returning to their own land when King
Cyrus gave them permission to do so. But who can say
that Haman would not have pursued them there as well?

We know from the Scriptures that in the days of Daniel
the Chaldeans came near and accused the Jews because
they would not fall down and worship the golden image
which King Nebuchadnezzar had set up. As a result Sha-
drach, Meshach, and Abednego were cast into the midst
of a burning fiery furnace which had actually been heated
seven times more than usual. The story of their miracu-

lous deliverance is so well known that we need not repeat it here. We merely point out that the anti-Semitism which flared up in the days of Mordecai and Esther was not a new thing. Indeed, it looks as though Mordecai may have had all of this before him when he refused to bow down to Haman. Thus we see that even though he and his compatriots did not return to their own land when they had the opportunity to do so, the Lord made even that to work out for their good and His glory.

Further evidence that Mordecai had no desire to hide his grief is seen in the fact that he "came even before the king's gate," which none could enter who were clothed with sackcloth. Thank God, such is not the case with the King of kings! The child of God is bidden to come boldly to His throne of grace in order that he may obtain mercy and find grace to help in time of need (Heb. 4:16). But even though Mordecai could not come to the throne of King Ahasuerus, he went as far as he could. And in so doing he was really representing many others. "In every province, whithersoever the king's commandment and his decree came, there was great mourning among the Jews, and fasting, and weeping, and wailing: and many lay in sackcloth and ashes."

News of all this finally reached Queen Esther. But it was not Mordecai who informed her. It was her own "maids and her chamberlains" who came and told her, and she was "exceedingly grieved." The chamberlains here referred to were eunuchs appointed by the king to wait on her. But it looks as though neither the maids nor the chamberlains took the time to find out just why Mordecai was in trouble. Neither did the queen inquire at first. All she did was to send "raiment to clothe Mordecai, and to take away his sackcloth from him: but he received it not." Trouble such as he had was not to be cured by a

mere change of raiment. In the light of what our Lord
Jesus said in His Sermon on the Mount about fasting, it
may be thought that Mordecai should have received this
change of raiment from the queen. But our Lord was not
speaking of true mourners when He said, "When ye fast,
be not, as the hypocrites, of a sad countenance: for they
disfigure their faces, that they may appear unto men
to fast." Mordecai was no hypocrite.

The Lord Jesus did say, however, that "thou, when
thou fastest, anoint thine head, and wash thy face; that
thou appear not unto men to fast, but unto thy Father
which is in secret: and thy Father, which seeth in secret,
shall reward thee openly" (Matt. 6:17, 18). And even
though Mordecai was no hypocrite, he did not rise to such
triumphant heights as those indicated in the words of our
Lord Jesus. Such conduct is possible only when one is in
full fellowship with the Lord. And since His holy name
is not even mentioned by Mordecai, we must conclude
that he could hardly attain to the standards set by our
Lord in His sermon. Then, too, he lived in an age when
the light of the glorious Gospel had not yet dawned.
Therefore, we could hardly expect him to see things as we
may see them now. So, instead of condemning him for
not doing better than he did, it might be well for us to
ask ourselves how we measure up to the light which we
have.

It was Mordecai's refusal to receive the change of raiment from the queen that led her to send one of the king's
chamberlains to "know what it was, and why it was" that
he acted this way. "So Hatach went forth to Mordecai
unto the street of the city, which was before the king's
gate." Apparently, the king's decree had not been published within the palace itself. If it had, then surely
Hatach, and even the queen, would have known some-

thing about the cause of Mordecai's grief and sorrow. It is quite possible that even Haman did not realize that what he had done would affect anyone in the palace, much less the queen herself. As a matter of fact, that that was the case is shown by the discovery which he was to make later. And that reminds us of a statement made by the Apostle Paul in his letter to the Corinthians. In speaking of the wisdom of God he said that none of the princes of this world knew it, for had they known it, they would not have crucified the Lord of glory (I Cor. 2:8). No doubt Satan knows a great deal, but he is not omniscient. And in spite of many defeats he tries again and again to destroy that which is indestructible. Long before the days of Mordecai the Lord had said of Israel, "No weapon that is formed against thee shall prosper" (Isa. 54:17). And that which we are considering just now in the Book of Esther is a good illustration of this.

In the public square which was before the king's gate Mordecai told Hatach "all that had happened unto him, and of the sum of the money that Haman had promised to pay to the king's treasuries for the Jews, to destroy them." Inasmuch as Haman, in his conference with the king, had merely stated that there was "a certain people" which it was "not for the king's profit to suffer," or permit to exist, this information would clear up any doubt which there may have been as to the identity of that "certain people." Moreover, the fact that a sum of money was involved would also serve to answer any question that might arise concerning the king's readiness to grant Haman's request. It was "the king's profit," and not Haman's hatred of Mordecai which was made the excuse for this murderous plot. To confirm all of this information Mordecai gave Hatach "the copy of the writing of the decree that was given at Shushan to destroy them."

This was documentary evidence right from headquarters.

Hatach was not only to deliver this document to Queen Esther, he was "to declare it unto her." That meant, so I take it, that he was to explain it to her carefully. It is not to be supposed, of course, that she could not read it for herself. In declaring the matter Hatach would make it very clear to her that she herself was involved, as well as Mordecai, and the rest of the Jews. We may well imagine what a surprise that would be to her. The laws of the Medes and the Persians had the reputation of being immutable. And the royal seal that made this decree effective was none other than that of Ahasuerus himself.

In view of all this, Mordecai's charge must have sounded bold indeed. The charge was that she was to go unto the king "to make supplication unto him, and to make request before him for her people." Mordecai did not even suggest an alternative. Neither did he make it optional with her. It was that, or else. "And Hatach came and told Esther the words of Mordecai." Little did she dream what she asked for when she sent Hatach "to know what it was, and why it was"! Notwithstanding, it would afford her a most unusual opportunity to use her royal office for the salvation of thousands of her people.

As we reflect on that, we feel constrained to point out a lesson for all us here. As Christians we have been brought to royal estate through the grace of our Lord Jesus Christ. Some of our fellow Christians who "have obtained like precious faith with us" (II Peter 1:1) are this very day being persecuted for His name's sake. And we are clearly taught in the Word of God that if one member of the Body of Christ suffer, all the members suffer with it (I Cor. 12:26). Therefore, when their cries for help come to us, it is really our duty to use our royal privileges in making intercession for them at the throne of grace. The ears of our Lord are always open to the cries of His own, and He heareth and delivereth them (Ps. 34:15, 17). And that was no mere theory with the psalmist for when he was "in a great strait" he said, "Let me fall now into the hand of the Lord; for very great are his mercies: but let me not fall into the hand of man" (I Chron. 21:13).

The Jews were certainly in the hands of men at that time. But He who delivered them into the hands of men, in order to chasten them, did not cease to care for them. And it is with much interest that we see Him work here even though He is not once named. He allowed things to come to such a pass that even the most sanguine might give up in despair. But it is just at that point that He intervenes for their deliverance.

So far as Esther herself is concerned, it seems that she saw no farther than the king. Note how often she mentions him in her message to Mordecai. She commands Hatach to say: "All the *king's* servants, and the people of the *king's* provinces, do know, that whosoever, whether man or woman, shall come unto the *king* into the inner court, who is not called, there is one law of his to put him to death, except such to whom the *king* shall hold out the golden scepter, that he may live: but I have not been called to come in unto the *king* these thirty days." But "the king's heart is in the hand of the Lord, as the rivers of water: he turneth it whithersoever he will" (Prov. 21:1). What a comfort it would have been to Esther if, in faith, she had recognized that fact at this point! Then, instead of having her eyes on a mere man, she would have endured as seeing Him who is invisible. (See Heb. 11:27.)

When her message came to Mordecai he lost no time in replying by saying, "Think not with thyself that thou shalt escape in the king's house, more than all the Jews."

If she had any feeling of personal security because of her exalted position, she must have received quite a shock when she heard that in this particular circumstance she would be no better off than the rest of the Jews. Evidently, the edict made no exceptions. But she was not to consider that a calamity, but an opportunity to use her royal position in a most wonderful way.

From the words of Mordecai we gather that he believed that deliverance would come, if not through Esther then through someone else. Said he to her, "If thou altogether holdest thy peace at this time, then shall there enlargement and deliverance arise to the Jews from another place." We may well wish that he had made that more personal than he did. When he said "another place" he spoke after the manner of those who in our own times talk about Heaven helping those who cannot help themselves. Surely, he must have known that well-known verse which says, "My help cometh from the Lord, which made heaven and earth" (Ps. 121:2). And that is bound to mean a great deal more to a soul in trouble than a mere place.

Previous to this Mordecai had charged Esther not to make known her people or her kindred. This is referred to twice in one chapter (Esther 2:10, 20). But the picture had changed a good deal since then. This was no time for silence. The time had come to speak out boldly and conceal nothing. As we have seen, Mordecai was sure that enlargement, or relief, would come. But he warned Esther that neither she nor her father's house would share in it if she did not act now. That sounds as if he believed that she would be specially punished for her failure to do what she could for her people at that time. But then he did not stop at that. Said he, "Who knoweth whether thou art come to the kingdom for such a time as this?"

Perhaps there is no verse in all the Book of Esther

which is referred to more often than this one. And one can see that such a suggestion would be far more powerful than all the threats that he might make. She probably never thought of herself as a woman of destiny. But she was. If she had not come to the kingdom for such a time as that, we would never have heard of her. Adapting a text from another part of Scripture we might say, "There were many maidens in Israel in those days and yet to none of them did this opportunity come, save to Esther."

Whether it was this challenge, or whether it was fear for her own life that moved Esther, we do not know. But she did as Mordecai bade her. Nevertheless, she had her own idea about the way it should be done. So she "bade them return Mordecai this answer, Go, gather together all the Jews that are present in Shushan, and fast ye for me, and neither eat nor drink three days, night or day; I also and my maidens will fast likewise; and so will I go in unto the king, which is not according to the law: and if I perish, I perish."

Evidently this plan met with the approval of Mordecai because we read that he went his way and did according to all that Esther had commanded him. We have no way of knowing how many Jews there may have been in Shushan at that time. The number must have run into the hundreds because we learn from chapter 9 of this same book that they slew about eight hundred of their enemies in the palace and the city. It would take quite a force to accomplish such a feat. However much they may have been separated from each other before for one reason or another, the fact that they faced a common foe united them as nothing else could.

It seems fair enough to conclude that the three days of fasting may have had some religious significance even though that is not mentioned here. We remember that

David was in a great strait after he had sinned in numbering the people, and he was offered "either *three* years' famine; or *three* months to be destroyed before thy foes, while that the sword of thine enemies overtaketh thee; or else *three* days the sword of the Lord" (I Chron. 21:12). He chose the last because, as we have already seen, he would rather fall into the hand of the Lord than into the hands of men.

Queen Esther apparently had no such faith. Her final word to Mordecai was, "If I perish, I perish." She was resigned to her fate, as men would say. For her, everything depended on whether or not the king would hold out the golden scepter to her. "No other writer tells us of this custom, but it is in perfect harmony with oriental habits and modes of thought. Some have objected that the king would not always have a golden scepter by him; but the Persepolitan sculptures uniformly represent him with a long staff in his hand, which is probably the scepter" (*Pulpit Commentary*). Legally, Esther had no right to enter the royal presence unless called. But she had "not been called to come in unto the king these thirty days." That was why she said, "If I perish, I perish."

At this point the sacred historian notes very simply that "Mordecai went his way, and did according to all that Esther had commanded him." He seems not to be at all anxious about the outcome. And while it is true that nothing is said here about his faith in God, nevertheless, he behaved like one who has faith. And in that regard he stands out in contrast to Esther who apparently was none too hopeful at this point. It was truly a dark hour for all the Jews. But that also meant that the dawn of a better day was not far off.

## Chapter 5

# AN AUDIENCE WITH THE KING

WE ARE SO ACCUSTOMED to arranging interviews by mail or telephone, or through some mutual friend, that all of the details of this chapter may seem to be quite unnecessary and tedious. But we have to remember that here we are in an oriental court. Things were done differently there at that time. Indeed, one does not have to go that far back or that far away to find people who still follow much the same procedure in their regular life. Americans traveling in countries to the south of our own find that the people there have ways of doing things that are quite different from our hasty habits.

The writer well remembers one occasion in Palestine when he wanted to make certain purchases before leaving there for England and home. Not knowing the Arabic language, he was glad to avail himself of the kind services of a Christian lady in Jerusalem who not only knew the language but also the customs of the people. Together we went to the business section of the old city of Jerusalem. There we found exactly what was wanted, and it seemed as though it should take only a few minutes to complete the purchase and be on our way. But I soon discovered that that would not have been the proper thing to do. So we sat down and talked quite leisurely about the business in hand. When we inquired about the price, it seemed to be quite exorbitant. But my friend assured me that that need not disturb me.

After some more talk, the price was reduced to a point where I was quite ready to close the deal. But my friend urged more patience. And while we were discussing the matter, a servant brought in some coffee for us to sip meanwhile. Then, after more bargaining, we finally arrived at the point where all concerned seemed to be quite satisfied. The deal was closed, and we prepared to leave. We were showered with words of thanks and appreciation on the part of the proprietor who appeared to have enjoyed the whole occasion even more than we had.

As we left there that morning, we recalled the story of Abraham's purchase of the cave of Machpelah as recorded in Genesis 23. His wife Sarah had died, and he wanted to buy a place to bury her remains. Under such circumstances it might have seemed proper to dispense with formality. But we find as we read the story that such was not to be the case. Even in a time of sorrow and bereavement, things must be done according to the custom of the country. And I think that most of us will agree that there are things which must be done in a quiet and deliberate way if we are to derive the greatest possible blessing from them. That that was the case in the matter we are now considering in the Book of Esther is clearly shown in the sequel to this. If Esther had rushed through this whole affair, she probably would never have achieved her purpose.

Esther's preparation for her audience with the king may also teach us a lesson. For three days she fasted with her maidens. Whether or not she was clothed in sackcloth like the rest of the Jews, we are not told. But that would be not at all unlikely. In any case, we are told that she put on her royal apparel. She knew perfectly well that no one might enter the king's presence dressed in sackcloth. As a matter of fact, she probably had no desire to appear before him that way.

In keeping with his station, as well as her own, she dressed up like a queen. She was going to have an audience with the king. That in itself would indicate the manner in which she should dress. Even though she came as a suppliant, she never lost sight of the fact that it was the king himself who had promoted her to the place of honor she was privileged to occupy at that time. And should we do less when we come to have an audience with the King of kings? Has He not lifted us as beggars from the dunghill to set us among princes? (See I Sam. 2:8.) And has He not provided us with the royal garments of salvation which are suited to His holy presence? (Cf. Matt. 22:12.) And therefore we may sing with one of old, "I will greatly rejoice in the Lord, my soul shall be joyful in my God; for he hath clothed me with the garments of salvation, he hath covered me with the robe of righteousness, as a bridegroom decketh himself with ornaments, and as a bride adorneth herself with her jewels" (Isa. 61:10).

Then notice the gradual way in which Esther approached the royal presence. She took her stand, first of all, "in the inner court of the king's house, over against the king's house." Her visit was well timed. "The king sat upon his royal throne, over against the gate of the house." If she had planned for this months in advance, it could not have been more favorably arranged. And is not that another evidence of the providence of God? And even though Ahasuerus be but a heathen king, he may serve us here as an illustration of the One who is always in readiness to receive us when we draw near to His throne.

"And it was so, when the king saw Esther the queen

standing in the court, that she obtained favor in his sight: and the king held out to Esther the golden scepter that was in his hand." It is written, "The king's wrath is as the roaring of a lion; but his favor is as the dew upon the grass" (Prov. 19:12). Esther feared the former, but, by God's grace, she experienced the latter. Those three days of fasting and waiting were not in vain.

It may be thought strange that Esther should chose this method of gaining an audience with the king. After all, she was his wife. But we must not judge her conduct by modern standards, but according to those which were observed in those days. The history of those times confirms the fact that she followed the only course that was open to her. There was no alternative. Mordecai had not specified how she was to approach the king. She had to work that out herself. But the results prove that she made no mistake. And we may well imagine the relief that was hers as she drew near and touched the top of the extended scepter, undoubted token of the royal favor.

"Then said the king unto her, What wilt thou, queen Esther? and what is thy request? it shall be even given thee to the half of the kingdom." He sensed immediately that this was something more than a formal call. Nobody could have realized more than he that Esther had actually risked her life in order to secure this brief interview. Only a matter of grave importance could induce one to do that. By extending his scepter, and in addressing her as queen, he made her doubly sure that he was ready to listen to her request.

Note that he does not say, "What have you to tell me?" He was not only in the listening mood, he was in the giving mood. He was ready to grant her request even to the half of his kingdom. Perhaps we should not take that statement too literally. We have a similar case in the

New Testament where Herod promised the daughter of
Herodias anything that she might ask of him even to the
half of his kingdom. But when she asked for the head
of John the Baptist we read that "the king was exceeding
sorry" (Mark 6:26). That head was worth more than all
of his little kingdom. But evidently he never thought
of that.

Queen Esther might have asked for the head of Haman
right then and there. But the time had not yet come for
that. So she simply replies, "If it seem good unto the
king, let the king and Haman come this day unto the
banquet that I have prepared for him." It is of deep interest to note that she makes this altogether a matter of
the king's pleasure. Haman's pleasure or convenience
was not even mentioned. She had prepared this banquet,
not for Haman, but for the king. And the fact that she
spoke of the banquet as already prepared is also very interesting.

In view of this, it is difficult to think that there was no
faith there. She must have believed that somehow her
request would be granted. Oh, that we had similar faith
when we come to the Lord with our petitions! And this
is the more remarkable because it was only three days
before this that she had said, "If I perish, I perish." Evidently those days of fasting were also days of reflection.
It takes more than abstinence from food to produce so
profound a change as this. And we like to think that
even though the Lord is not mentioned by name here,
nevertheless, His Holy Spirit was quietly working in the
heart and mind of Esther.

In contrast to the quiet and deliberate manner of
Queen Esther, we hear the king saying, "Cause Haman
to make haste, that he may do as Esther hath said. So
the king and Haman came to the banquet that Esther

had prepared." Whatever other business the king may have had, all was put to one side in favor of such business as the queen might have. A man in his position could easily have found some good reason for not attending a banquet that day. No doubt matters of state would be awaiting his attention all the time. But once again we see the hand of God clearing the way for His child. All of the affairs of the Persian Empire are only as "a drop of a bucket, and are counted as the small dust of the balance" (Isa. 40:15) by "the everlasting God, the Lord, the Creator of the ends of the earth." And yet He upon whom the universe depends is never too busy to receive us and to hear us as we make known to Him our petitions.

At the banquet again it was the king who took the initiative when he asked Esther, "What is thy petition?" And again he repeated the promise that her request would be granted even to the half of his kingdom. But this time all of this took place in the hearing of Haman. Knowing something of the urgency of the matter in hand, we cannot but marvel at the self-restraint of Esther. The king had left the door wide open, so to speak. But her only request just now is that the king and Haman should come to the banquet that she was going to prepare for them on the morrow. At that time she would finally make known her request.

Little did any present at that banquet that day realize how this postponement was going to work to the advantage of Esther. What if she had been in a hurry? When she postponed her request she did better than she knew. Of course, it may be argued that it was nothing but fear that held her back. The request she was to make involved the king's favorite who was the guest of honor at that banquet. Hatach had brought her the information from Mordecai that "Haman had promised to pay to the king's treasuries for the Jews, to destroy them." It is not difficult to imagine how we would feel if we were face to face with one who had plotted to destroy our loved ones. When she thought of the high position he now occupied in the kingdom, it might well make her pause. But if she had any fears she did not manifest them. Wonderful things were to happen within the next few hours which would abundantly justify Esther's course at this time. But of them she knew nothing at the moment.

Evidently Haman never suspected what was in store for him either. He "went forth that day joyful and with a glad heart." But his joy was soon clouded. When he "saw Mordecai in the king's gate, that he stood not up, nor moved for him, he was full of indignation against Mordecai." It is indeed amazing that a man of Mordecai's humble standing should cause so much disturbance. To all outward appearances he had neither social position nor political power. And yet his attitude toward Haman is the cause of trouble which soon affects hundreds, if not thousands, of others. It may be that Haman saw in him something more than a mere porter at the gate of Ahasuerus. For some reason or other he may have considered him as one who occupied a key position, as we would say nowadays. And in that respect he may be typical of the Jewish people. Their importance in the world today is out of all proportion to their total number as compared with the population of the world, or even of any particular country. There must be a reason for that.

If the wise men who came from the East when Christ was born had asked, "Where is He that is born king of the Egyptians?" or, "Where is He that is born king of the Grecians?" their question would probably have stirred up but little interest. But when they asked, "Where is he that is born king of the Jews?" Herod was troubled, and all

Jerusalem with him. And the flight into Egypt was ordered because Herod sought the young Child to destroy Him. (See Matt. 2:13.) Haman's hatred of Mordecai, and his plot to destroy him and his people, are just episodes in a program of destruction that began when Cain murdered his brother Abel. That program will find its great climax in the Tribulation when the dragon, that is Satan, makes war with the remnant of Israel with a view to their total annihilation. (See Rev. 12:9-17.) Of course, we are not suggesting for one moment that Haman was aware of all this. He was but the instrument for the time being of "that old serpent, the devil," who knew full well that out of "the people of Mordecai" was to come the One who would seal his doom.

As for Haman, we read that he "refrained himself." Apparently he never let on as he passed through the gate that day that he had even noticed that Mordecai did not rise up to honor him. After all he was next to the king and it would never do for him to explode in public. Moreover, it would have hampered him greatly in his plan to destroy all the Jews if he had manifested his anger then and there. Like the one whom he was serving, he was far too astute for that. But to provide himself with an escape from all of this, when he came home "he sent and called for his friends, and Zeresh his wife, and Haman told them of the glory of his riches, and the multitude of his children, and all the things wherein the king had promoted him, and how he had advanced him above the princes and servants of the king."

To most of us this would have been quite nauseating. But there are those who can listen to such bombast and actually applaud a man who invites people to a party at his home just to listen to him brag about all that he has. To cap it all, he mentions the fact that Esther the queen had not permitted anyone to attend the banquet that she had prepared that day except himself. And he hastens to add, "Tomorrow am I invited unto her also with the king." But there was just one thing that spoiled it all so far as he was concerned. "All this availeth me nothing, so long as I see Mordecai the Jew sitting at the king's gate." It is clear that the emphasis here is on the word "sitting." Haman does not go into detail. But it must have been plain to all of his guests that the thing that bothered him was the fact that Mordecai remained seated as Haman passed by. It was more than his pride could take.

"Then said Zeresh his wife and all his friends unto him, Let a gallows be made of fifty cubits high, and tomorrow speak thou unto the king that Mordecai may be hanged thereon: then go thou in merrily with the king unto the banquet." This ready suggestion so unanimously agreed upon will give us some idea of how cheap human life can be. But there was no thought of disposing of Mordecai quietly. Inasmuch as the Persians did not execute criminals by hanging them, it is thought the word for *gallows* here should be rendered *a pale* or *a cross*. It was by impalement that the Persians punished rebels and traitors in those days. (See Esther 2:23.)

The fact that this "gallows" was to be fifty cubits high, or about 75 feet, has led some commentators to believe that there may be some error in the text. Inasmuch as letters were used in place of numbers, that would not be impossible. But it might also mean that the pale, or cross, was to be placed in some prominent place, high up so that all might see it. That such was the case when our blessed Lord was crucified is quite generally held by most Christians, even though the Scriptures do not actually say that it was on "a hill far away." In any case, it does look as though they would make a public example of Mordecai. No doubt this was calculated to strike terror to the hearts of the rest of the Jews. But so far as Haman was concerned, he could then go in merrily with the king to the banquet. With Mordecai out of the way the main obstacle to his happiness would be eliminated. And no doubt there were those who thought that by crucifying the Lord Jesus they could get rid of Him also. But it has not worked out that way.

Nevertheless, "the thing pleased Haman; and he caused the gallows to be made." Little did he dream that he was really preparing for his own execution. But he is not the only one who will one day discover that his final doom is really one of his own making. Despising the riches of God's goodness and forbearance and longsuffering, men today treasure up to themselves "wrath against the day of wrath and revelation of the righteous judgment of God; who will render to every man according to his deeds" (Rom. 2:4-6).

## Chapter 6

# THE RISE AND FALL OF MEN

THE READER OF HISTORY cannot fail to notice that history is made up largely of the rise and fall of nations as well as of the rise and fall of individuals. The historical books of the Bible give many illustrations of this fact. But they do more, they also give us the moral reason for this. The Bible tells us that "God is the judge: he putteth down one, and setteth up another" (Ps. 75:7). The great King Nebuchadnezzar had to learn that by bitter experience. Even though he was declared to be that "head of gold" (Dan. 2:38), the first and greatest of a long line of emperors, he had to learn that it was the God of Heaven who had given him "a kingdom, power, and strength, and glory." As a matter of fact, he learned even more than that through the humbling experience of having to live in the open fields like a beast for seven years. It was at the end of those days that he lifted up his eyes to Heaven, and his understanding returned unto him, and then he blessed the Most High, and praised and honored Him who lives forever, who not only rules among men on the earth, but who also "doeth according to his will in the army of heaven . . . and none can stay his hand, or say unto him, What doest thou?" (Dan. 4:34, 35).

The chapter now before us gives us another striking illustration of this. In our study of chapter 3 we saw the promotion, or advancement, of Haman. We also saw that instead of using that advancement for the good and blessing of others, he became proud and haughty. How truly does the Bible say, "Pride goeth before destruction, and an haughty spirit before a fall" (Prov. 16:18)! And "when pride cometh, then cometh shame" (Prov. 11:2). Our present chapter gives abundant proof of the truth of these statements. On the other hand, our chapter also gives us a good illustration of the text which says, "Them that honor me I will honor" (I Sam. 2:30).

The manner in which God moves to bring these things to pass is full of interest. We may have wondered why Esther was so slow in presenting her real request to the king when she had the opportunity to do so. We have suggested that that was quite in keeping with the manner of the Orient. But there is more to it than that. The hand of the Lord was in that apparent delay. It was all part of His divine plan to humble the proud and arrogant Haman. Of course, He might have used some other method. He could have smitten Haman with some fatal illness, or He might have brought upon him some other adversity. But if He had, then some might have explained his downfall as nothing more or less than an unhappy circumstance, something which might have happened to anyone else.

The action begins in the bedchamber of the king himself. "On that night could not the king sleep." Nothing is said about the cause of his insomnia. It is written, "The sleep of a laboring man is sweet, whether he eat little or much: but the abundance of the rich will not suffer him to sleep" (Eccles. 5:12). Now if this Ahasuerus was the wealthy Xerxes of secular history, it is quite possible that the abundance of his riches did not permit him to sleep. How different was the case of the Psalmist who said, "I will not give sleep to mine eyes, or slumber to mine eyelids, until I find out a place for the Lord, an habitation for the mighty God of Jacob" (Ps. 132:4, 5)! We may be sure that it was no such glorious purpose as this that kept Ahasuerus awake that night. He who neither slumbers nor sleeps (Ps. 121:3, 4), the ever watchful Keeper of Israel, was present in the royal bedchamber that night. The king's heart is in His hand to turn it whithersoever He wills (Prov. 21:1). In the case of Nebuchadnezzar, He used dreams "wherewith his spirit was troubled, and his sleep brake from him" (Dan. 2:1). And in the case of Darius whose "sleep went from him" (Dan. 6:18), we see again the hand of that same One who ever keepeth watch above His own.

Presumably sedatives were not unknown in those days. But Ahasuerus did not order one. He called in no physician to prescribe for him, nor a minstrel to play for him. "He commanded to bring the book of records of the chronicles; and they were read before the king." "It has been a custom with Eastern kings, in all ages, frequently to cause the annals of the kingdom to be read to them. It is resorted to, not merely to while away the tedium of an hour, but a source of instruction to the monarch, by reviewing the important incidents of his own life, as well as those of his ancestors" (*Jamieson, Fausset and Brown*). "And it was found written, that Mordecai had told of Bigthana and Teresh, two of the king's chamberlains, the keepers of the door, who sought to lay hand on the king Ahasuerus." We know from our study of chapter 2 that Ahasuerus knew all about this at the time it happened. But for some reason or other he did nothing to reward Mordecai then. And yet, in a sense, Ahasuerus owed his very life to Mordecai. In that sense he was his savior, even though he was not recognized as such.

How true it is that there are many today who have been saved from something worse than Ahasuerus was saved from, but they seem to know little or nothing about their Saviour! Apparently they just take Him for granted. They seem to be quite satisfied with what He has done for them. They may even sing about it at times. But they forget that, according to the Bible, salvation is something more than a great work which has been wrought for us. When the aged Simeon gazed into the face of the Babe Jesus he said to God, "Mine eyes have seen thy salvation" (Luke 2:30). Apparently, to him at least, salvation was more than something, it was Someone.

The rediscovery of Mordecai by Ahasuerus may well serve to teach all of us who claim to be saved how important it is to get better acquainted with the One who has saved us. He has not only saved us from the eternal consequences of our sins, but He saves us moment by moment as we walk through a world that is filled with perils and dangers, seen and unseen. Oh, that there were more searching of "the book of the records" so that we might become increasingly aware of this and, like Ahasuerus, do something about it! It was a night well spent to look up some of these things. Then it would not have to be said of our blessed Lord, as I fear that it must be said so far as some of us are concerned, "There is nothing done for him." Just as Ahasuerus inquired, "What honor and dignity hath been done to Mordecai for this?" so also may we inquire concerning our Lord Jesus, "What honor and dignity have I brought to Him who has done so much for me?" God forbid that it should ever have to be said of any of us that we have done nothing for Him!

At this point it is interesting to observe that just as the king was preparing to honor Mordecai, the enemy of Mordecai arrived on the scene. Such a coincidence is striking, but it is not unique. We need not suppose, of course, that Haman was aware of what was going on. But the one of whom he is a type is very wise. Satan will always seek to prevent, if possible, the honoring of any of God's saints. And he will certainly do all in his power also to keep you and me from bringing honor to the name of the Lord Jesus. It is in view of this that Haman's arrival at the court of Ahasuerus at this time is very significant. He probably had passed a sleepless night also. His workmen must have been busy most of the night preparing the gallows on which he hoped to hang Mordecai the next day. All he needed now was the royal permission to carry out his nefarious plan. He was "all set," as men would say today.

It seems that Haman must have made known his presence in some way or another. In any case, the king seems to be aware that someone is in the court and accordingly he asks, "Who is in the court?" "And the king's servants said unto him, "Behold, Haman standeth in the court. And the king said, Let him come in." Apparently, Haman did not have to go through the formality of waiting for the extended scepter as did Queen Esther. At least, nothing is said about that here. On the other hand, neither did the king give him a chance to present his request to him. The king did not treat him as a suppliant but as an adviser. And so, without even waiting to say, "Good morning," he says to Haman, "What shall be done unto the man whom the king delighteth to honor?"

We note that the king did not explain to Haman why he was asking him this question. He gave no hint of "the man" whom he had in mind. And Haman was so self-occupied that he did not inquire who it might be. With utter selfishness he "thought in his heart, To whom would the king delight to do honor more than to myself?"

His pride robbed him of ordinary prudence, as it so often does. And so, once again we see the hand of the Lord who "taketh the wise in their own craftiness" (Job 5:13 and I Cor. 3:19). Thus the question put to Haman by the king only served to bring out more than ever the selfishness that was in his heart. It is very clear that he knew nothing at all of that spirit manifested by the Apostle Paul who esteemed others better than himself (Phil. 2:3). His pride and his selfishness were his undoing.

In his ready reply to the king he shows no reserve whatsoever. He covets the habiliments of royalty itself. "For the man whom the king delighteth to honor" he would have them bring forth not only royal apparel, but "the royal apparel which the king useth to wear." Neither did he want a horse like the king's horse but the very "horse that the king rideth upon." And then to cap it all, he suggests "the crown royal which is set upon his head." Moreover, these things were to "be delivered to the hand of one of the king's most noble princes." No ordinary chamberlain, or valet, would be good enough to "array the man withal whom the king delighteth to honor."

Then, to complete the picture, they were to bring "the man" on horseback through the street of the city with a herald proclaiming before him, "Thus shall it be done to the man whom the king delighteth to honor." Little did Haman dream that such was not to be his honor. Blinded by pride, he could see no one but himself in that place of honor. On the other hand, we suspect that the king must have known all the while that Haman was really speaking for himself in this matter. If that were the case, then we can see that there must have been a bit of humor in all of this, sad as it is otherwise.

In his reply to Haman we note that the king said nothing about the crown royal. If he had granted that, we can see that it might have been assumed by some that Ahasuerus had actually transferred his royal authority and dignity to another. Indeed, it is entirely possible that Haman himself would have assumed that. One as selfish as he would have stopped at nothing short of the throne itself.

What follows here is most dramatic. "Then the king said to Haman, Make haste, and take the apparel and the horse, as thou hast said, and do even so to Mordecai the Jew, that sitteth at the king's gate: let nothing fail of all that thou hast spoken." We wonder whether Haman displayed any emotion when he heard that statement. Nothing is said about that here. But knowing something of the real purpose for which he had come to the palace that morning, one wonders how he could control himself so well at this time. Whatever his feelings were, he did not debate the matter with the king. He did not even beg to be excused. We may be sure that he would have done so had he dared.

"Then took Haman the apparel and the horse, and arrayed Mordecai, and brought him on horseback through the street of the city, and proclaimed before him, Thus shall it be done unto the man whom the king delighteth to honor." He had repeated those last words so often in the presence of the king that by this time he must have been able to repeat them quite readily. According to the commandment of the king, he was to let nothing fail of all that he had spoken. He dared not disobey even though to obey meant that he had to eat his own words, as it were.

But what about Mordecai? So far as the record goes, he received all of this in silence. No doubt he, too, must have been somewhat surprised at the turn which events had taken, quite as much as Haman was. But then, we remember that he had said to Esther that deliverance would arise. And in that which Haman was ordered to do to him he probably saw the beginning of the fulfillment of that prediction of his. And in all of this we may see a foreshadowing of what Satan himself will yet have to do when he is made to bow the knee before our Lord Jesus. And not only that, the Lord has promised His own that He will make them of the synagogue of Satan come and worship before their feet, and to make them know that He has loved His own (Rev. 3:9).

The patience and faithfulness of Mordecai was abundantly rewarded. What if he had weakened before that and had yielded to Haman? Think of what he would have lost! And in saying that, we are not thinking only of the temporal honor bestowed upon Mordecai. In a much higher sense the Lord was honoring one who had honored Him. And the very fact that he received all of this in silence is very significant. He had nothing to boast of in himself. His behavior would seem to indicate that he recognized that. His conduct all through was certainly exemplary. He did not allow these things to puff him up with pride. And we do well to follow his example. Haman's promotion, as we have seen, "went to his head," as the saying goes. Such was not the case with Mordecai. He would have been a fool indeed if he had not profited by the very thing which he saw to be the ruin of his enemy. And so, with becoming grace and modesty, he carried his honors well. And when the procession was all over "Mordecai came again to the king's gate." Apparently, he resumed his former position as if he had been used merely as an illustration of one "whom the king delighteth to honor."

"But Haman hasted to his house mourning, and having his head covered." The head covering he used was probably a veil which was a mark of mourning in those days.

For example, we read in Jeremiah 14:3 that the nobles of Judah sent "their little ones to the waters: they came to the pits, and found no water; they returned with their vessels empty; they were ashamed and confounded, and covered their heads." In like manner David, fleeing from Jerusalem because of his son Absalom, "wept as he went up, and had his head covered, and he went barefoot" (II Sam. 15:30). All of those who fled with him did the same. From these references we gather that it was the usual mark of mourning in those days in that part of the world. And it would be a sign to the family of Haman that something dreadful had happened to the head of that household.

"And Haman told Zeresh his wife and all his friends every thing that had befallen him." It was a great contrast to what he had hoped to be able to tell them on his return from his visit to the palace. When he left them not many hours before, he was told by his wife to go merrily with the king to the banquet. That banquet was evidently postponed for a while in order to allow time for Haman to carry out the command of the king. It seems reasonable to suppose that an event such as we have been considering would be known to everyone in the palace. Esther must have heard about it. Perhaps she and her ladies saw the whole procession. And the same may be said for the family of Haman unless his house was too far away from the royal palace for them to be fully aware of all that had happened there that morning. According to the plan outlined by Zeresh, the wife of Haman, he was to speak to the king about hanging Mordecai and then to go merrily to the banquet arranged by Queen Esther. But as, in great detail, he reviewed all that had taken place that morning, it would be quite evident to all of them that things did not augur well for him.

"Then said his wise men and Zeresh his wife unto him, If Mordecai be the seed of the Jews, before whom thou hast begun to fall, thou shalt not prevail against him, but shalt surely fall before him." We are not told on what they based this statement. Since they must have known all along that Mordecai was a Jew, it does seem strange that they did not say anything about this before. This shows that people may be aware of certain things and yet not be affected by them until something unusual takes place. Then, all of a sudden their whole attitude changes. The same ones who were quite ready to urge the hanging of Mordecai, as if that were a very simple matter, now take the position that he is invincible. They do not even try to encourage Haman to believe that matters might turn out better than he had anticipated. They prophesied nothing but gloom. Haman had begun to fall, and nothing could now prevent his complete undoing. Such talk is characteristic of Satan and his agents. To begin with, they are ready with advice which promises complete success. But when their poor dupes discover that things have taken a turn against them, they have no message of hope and comfort, but only one of gloom and despair.

It may be that these lines are being read by one to whom Satan has promised much. Perhaps you have begun to realize already that you are doomed to disappointment. He did the same with Adam and Eve in the Garden of Eden. He promised them that if they ate the forbidden fruit, they would be as gods. But when they found themselves face to face with Him, whose one single commandment they had disobeyed when they listened to the voice of the tempter, the latter had not one word of comfort or counsel for them. We are not suggesting that if he had said anything like that, that it would have been any good. He is always a liar. It is only in the "good news" of the Gospel that we hear words of hope and salvation such as every poor, lost sinner needs. But Haman's friends had no such words for him.

"And while they were yet talking with him, came the king's chamberlains, and hasted to bring Haman unto the banquet that Esther had prepared." That was to be his last banquet. If he had waited for the chamberlains to bring him the day before, the whole story might have been different. But in the meantime the Lord had been working out His plans and His purposes. And as we have said before, Satan may be wise but he is not omniscient. Had he known the way things would turn out, he might have advised his poor slave quite differently.

But Haman had begun to fall, not only before Mordecai, but before the Lord who "is known by the judgment which he executeth; the wicked is snared in the work of his own hands" (Ps. 9:16). It is "a fearful thing to fall into the hands of the living God" (Heb. 10:31). And the story of Haman's downfall should be a warning and a lesson to all who imagine that they can defeat Him. On the other hand, we may also take comfort from the study of this chapter when we take into account the wonderful way in which the Lord vindicates His own who trust in Him even though their faith may be weak and faltering. It may be, as in the case of Mordecai, that their faith may not even be articulate. But He is the God who hears the groaning which cannot be uttered. And He is able to do exceeding abundantly above all that we ask (audibly), or think (inaudibly).

## Chapter 7

# THE SECOND BANQUET

IN OUR STUDY of chapter 5 we suggest that Queen Esther manifested much self-restraint in that she did not present her real request at the first banquet which she had prepared for the king and Haman. But it may also be that she had good scriptural precedent for what she did. There are a number of references in the Old Testament which show that the Lord Himself waited until "the second time" to make known His real reason for speaking to His own. For example, we read that "the angel of the Lord called unto Abraham out of heaven the second time" after he had offered up Isaac as the Lord commanded him. It was then that He said, "In blessing I will bless thee, and in multiplying I will multiply thy seed as the stars of heaven, and as the sand which is upon the sea shore; and thy seed shall possess the gate of his enemies; and in thy seed shall all the nations of the earth be blessed; because thou hast obeyed my voice" (Gen. 22:17, 18).

It is very interesting to note that when the Lord spoke to Abraham the first time, "the scripture, foreseeing that God would justify the heathen through faith, preached before the gospel unto Abraham, saying, In thee shall all nations be blessed" (Gal. 3:8). But when He spoke to him the second time, He made mention of the Seed "which is

78

Christ" (v. 16). And it was in direct connection with that
that He also said, "And thy seed shall possess the gate
of his enemies." It may be that Queen Esther had that
promise in mind when she approached her heathen hus-
band with the request which was to bring about a preview of that, as we shall see when we come to study the
next chapter of our book. However, we must not presume too much.

But before we leave the subject of "the second time,"
we might notice also the fact that it was "when Solomon
had finished the building of the house of the Lord . .
that the Lord appeared to Solomon *the second ti*
he had appeared to him at Gibeon. And the 
unto him, I have heard thy prayer and thy
that thou hast made before me; I ha
house, which thou hast built, to
forever; and mine eyes and min
perpetually." It was at that sam
to the promise made to David                              not
fail thee a man upon the thr                         .ngs 9:1-5).
If Solomon had walked as                    ..s ....her walked, "in
integrity of heart, and in              ...ness," he would have
inherited that promise and t..  "Man" whom we now
know as "the Son of David," might have been known as
the Son of Solomon.

In the day when that promise to David is fulfilled
"there shall be a root of Jesse, which shall stand for an
ensign of the people; to it shall the Gentiles seek; and
his rest shall be glorious. And it shall come to pass in
that day, that the Lord shall set his hand again *the
second time* to recover the remnant of his people, which
shall be left, from Assyria, and from Egypt, and from
Pathros, and from Cush, and from *Elam*, and from Shinar,
and from Hamath, and from the islands of the sea" (Isa.

11:10, 11). The fact that *Elam* is specially mentioned in
this prophecy in connection with *the second time* is of
more than passing interest when we take into account
the fact that the events which we are considering at
present, in the Book of Esther, took place in Elam. Just
how much Esther may have known about all of this we
may not be able to say. But we like to think that she had
some acquaintance with it. And if so, then the words,
*the second time,* would have more than ordinary significance for her. For those who would like to pursue this
interesting subject still further, we suggest a careful consideration of both Acts 7:13 and Hebrews 9:28.

"So the king and Haman came to banquet with Esther
the queen. And the king said again unto Esther on the
second day at the banquet of wine, What is thy petition,
queen Esther? and it shall be granted thee: and what is
thy request? and it shall be performed, even to the half of
the kingdom." Once again it is the king who takes the
initiative here. And we note also that he is more personal than he was when he made a similar offer at the
first banquet. Here he actually addresses her as "Queen
Esther." Now we have no desire to magnify insignificant
details, but we believe that there is something here which
is very precious. It recalls the fact that when our blessed
Lord called Mary by name that she recognized Him as
her Lord and Master (John 20:16). Previous to that she
merely supposed Him to be the gardener. But the Good
Shepherd "calleth his own sheep by name" (John 10:3).
And we all know something of the thrill it gives us when
we are thus recognized by others.

In addressing her as "Queen Esther," the king was
giving emphasis to her royal position. In other words, he
was not treating her as he might treat some ordinary subject, or one of his servants. In thus addressing her he was

tacitly inviting her to make her petition large. And since she was about to make the most important request anyone can make this side of eternity, this must have been very encouraging. She was not only coming to a king, she was coming to him as a queen. And best of all, it was he who called attention to that fact.

"Then Esther the queen answered and said, If I have found favor in thy sight, O king, and if it please the king, let my life be given me at my *petition*, and my people at my *request*." She took the king at his word, and that quite literally. That is why she repeated the very words which he used when he made the gracious offer to give her her heart's desire. Now it may be of interest to the reader to know something of the distinctive meaning of these words. The one is not a mere repetition, or synonym, of the other. The word *petition* comes from a root which means "to inquire" as if to ascertain the will and pleasure of the one to whom the petition is addressed. It also has in it the idea of demanding. The word *request* comes from a root which means "to search out, or strive after." And that reminds us of the man who was granted his request "because of his importunity" (Luke 11:8). It also reminds us of the apostle Paul who wrote to the Romans, saying, "I beseech you, brethren, for the Lord Jesus Christ's sake, and for the love of the Spirit, that ye *strive* together with me in your prayers to God for me; that I may be delivered from them that do not believe" (Rom. 15:30). Such comparisons show that basically prayer is a matter of ascertaining the will of the Lord, and then earnestly beseeching Him to grant that which is according to His will.

The reason for Queen Esther's earnestness is clearly seen in what follows. She and her people had been sold "to be destroyed, to be slain, and to perish." In saying that she was using the very words of the document which had been written by the king's scribes, sealed with the king's seal, and carried to the remotest corners of the Persian Empire by posts who were "hastened by the king's commandment" (Esther 3:13, 15). In saying "we are sold," she was referring, of course, to Haman's offer of ten thousand talents of silver "to bring it into the king's treasuries."

"But," she continued, "if we had been sold for bond-men and bondwomen, I had held my tongue, although the enemy could not countervail [or, compensate for] the king's damage." Evidently the Jews, even though they were a captive people at that time, were not looked upon as slaves. Presumably they had all of the privileges of free men and women. Esther indicates that they might have accepted a change of social status without protest. But such a change, she intimates, would not be for the king's advantage, but rather to the contrary. All of the money which Haman had promised to pay into the king's treasuries would not compensate for the loss that this would mean to the king.

There is much food for thought in that statement. The service of a slave can never be the same in value as that of a free man. And in saying that, we are not unmindful of the fact that again and again the apostle Paul referred to himself as a slave of the Lord Jesus Christ. But that was voluntary slavery, like that of the Hebrew who had the opportunity to go out free, but who preferred to accept the mark of perpetual servitude because of his love for his master, his wife, and his children (Exod. 21:2-6). The slavery to which Queen Esther referred was not after that order. Nor was that all that Haman desired. His purpose was not only to enslave the Jews but ultimately to exterminate them.

"Then the king Ahasuerus answered and said unto Esther the queen, Who is he, and where is he, that durst presume in his heart to do so?" Had she followed the course that Nathan did when he came to charge David with the crime of having murdered Uriah the Hittite, she would have said, "Thou art the man" (II Sam. 12:7). But she did not use that method even though we can see that it would have been justifiable. The king must have known that the document from which she had actually quoted in part was sealed with the royal seal. And that certainly involved him. But it was not necessary to go into that at this point.

"And Esther said, The adversary and enemy is this wicked Haman." Before ever she mentioned his name, she used three strong words to describe him. To begin with, he is "the adversary," a type of him who is our "adversary the devil," and who, "as a roaring lion, walketh about, seeking whom he may devour" (I Peter 5:8). He is also the "enemy," or one who hates the people of God. And as the "wicked one" he is the very antithesis of goodness. This last epithet is used in the New Testament to describe both Satan and the Antichrist (I John 2:13 and II Thess. 2:8). And in view of all that Haman had done and was attempting to do, we do not believe that this description of him was an overstatement.

"Then Haman was afraid before the king and the queen." And well he might be! In one fell stroke Esther had exposed the character of him who lay at table that day with the royal couple. She had also answered the king's double question, "Who is he, and where is he, that durst presume in his heart to do so?" He was right there in the palace which made it quite unnecessary to send anyone after him to discover him and to apprehend him. He had walked right into the trap from which there was now no escape.

The king was infuriated! Rising from the banquet of wine in his wrath he went into the palace garden. What his motive may have been for such a move at that time we are not told. It will be remembered that the court of that garden was the scene of the seven days' feast which the king made for "all the people that were present in Shushan the palace, both unto great and small" (Esther 1:5). But whatever his motive, it would give him time to think about the turn which events had taken within the last few hours. He could not help but see that he was implicated in it all even though he may have been led into it quite innocently. On the one hand, for a man in his position to be caught off his guard in this way must have been humiliating indeed. It does seem strange that he did not know until then that Esther was a Jewess. The discovery of that fact would certainly put him in a dilemma, there can be no doubt about that. On the other hand, he must have been thoroughly convinced that all that Esther had charged was true. He did not ask her to prove her statement. In her heart-moving plea for her life, she had used the very terminology of the document dictated by the despicable Haman.

In the meantime, "Haman stood up to make request for his life to Esther the queen; for he saw that there was evil determined against him by the king." He made no attempt to explain. Neither did he express any sorrow for what he had done. It was his own life, and only that, that he was concerned about. We do not read of one word of repentance. He did not even go as far as Judas did when he said, "I have sinned in that I have betrayed the innocent blood" (Matt. 27:4). It is quite likely that he had seen Ahasuerus in a fit of anger before. But this must have been different. And there was no mistaking the fact that this would not pass off after a brief interlude in the garden.

Apparently, Esther remained silent through all of this. Her case was now in the hands of the king. We read of no display of emotion on her part. If Haman thought that he could play on the sympathies and emotions of a woman, he was mistaken that time. All too soon, so far as he was concerned, "the king returned out of the palace garden into the place of the banquet of wine." For him it was no longer a banquet, it was just the place of the banquet. And what he saw when he returned only made matters worse. "Haman was fallen upon the bed whereon Esther was." Beside himself in his desperation when he realized that his own life was in jeopardy, the one who had so boldly planned the extermination of a race of people became a coward in the face of death.

The "bed whereon Esther was," was probably one of those beds, or couches, "of gold and silver," mentioned in Esther 1:6. It must be remembered that the Orientals did not sit at table as we do now. They reclined as did our blessed Lord and His disciples at the Last Supper. That will explain the presence of a "bed" in the banqueting house. Nevertheless, the king seems to have put the worst possible construction upon this act of Haman, for he said, "Will he force the queen also before me in the house?" Under other circumstances that might have been the case. The horrible sin of Absalom comes to mind here when, upon the advice of Ahithophel, he "went in unto his father's concubines in the sight of all Israel" (II Sam. 16:21). But such was not the case here.

However unjust this remark of Ahasuerus was, it had its due effect upon the servants standing by. "As the word went out of the king's mouth, they covered Haman's face." Apparently, Haman had not one friend in that court. At least, not one rose up to plead his case or even to suggest to the enraged monarch that his judgment was too harsh. The covering of Haman's face was the sign that he was doomed to die even though the king had not as yet pronounced the death sentence upon him.

It is at this point in the story that we learn of the presence of others in the banqueting house. Among these was Harbonah, one of "the seven chamberlains that served in the presence of Ahasuerus the king" (Esther 1:10). He was one of the group which was sent to bring in Queen Vashti to show the people and the princes her beauty. But this time he was about a different kind of business. And he showed that he had knowledge of what was going on in the house of Haman that night. He knew all about "the gallows fifty cubits high, which Haman had made for Mordecai, who had spoken good for the king." It is true that he did not do more than call attention to it. But that was all that was needed. And the fact that he mentioned Mordecai as the one for whom the gallows were being erected was also significant. Harbonah was here supplying information which Queen Esther might have used, had that been necessary, when she was pleading for her own life and for the lives of her people.

Haman did not get a trial by a jury of his peers. Neither were any other witnesses called. Esther had described him for what he was. And that was quite sufficient for the king. It was Harbonah who revealed the fact that Haman had actually planned to kill Mordecai before the date set by the decree to exterminate the Jews. But what he had planned for another, and that an innocent man, turned out to be the means of his own doom. When the

king heard of the gallows which he had prepared for
Mordecai, he thundered out, "Hang him thereon!" Thus
Haman fell into the very pit which he had digged for
another. How true is the proverb, "Whoso diggeth a pit
shall fall therein: and he that rolleth a stone, it will return upon him" (Prov. 26:27)! "For he shall have judgment without mercy, that hath showed no mercy" (James
2:13). In other words, "Whatsoever a man soweth, that
shall he also reap" (Gal. 6:7).

It is interesting to find that the word here used for
*gallows* in the Greek translation of the passage is the
same word which is used for the *cross* of our Lord Jesus
Christ in the Greek New Testament in such passages as
Acts 5:30; 10:39; and 13:29. It is also found in Galatians
3:13 and I Peter 2:24. The word *tree* in all of these passages refers to the *cross* on which our Lord Jesus was
crucified. But the same word is also used in Revelation
2:7 and 22:2, 14 in connection with "the tree of life." Like
Haman, we deserved to die that death of shame and loss.
But the Lord Jesus died there in our stead as our Substi-
tute. And thus the cross, or the tree, which was a curse
for Him becomes for us "the tree of life."

"Then was the king's wrath pacified." It subsided like
the waters of a flood subside. But the death of Christ did
something more for us than to cause the wrath of God
to subside. By means of that cross He "delivered us from
the wrath to come" (I Thess. 1:10). And because of that
we have peace with God through our Lord Jesus Christ.
That, of course, is something about which Haman knew
nothing at all. His plea for his life was silenced when
they covered his face and took him to his own home to
die. And that brings to mind the words of the Psalmist
who said, "I have seen the wicked in great power, and

spreading himself like a green bay tree. Yet he passed away, and, lo, he was not: yea, I sought him, but he could not be found. Mark the perfect man, and behold the upright: for the end of that man is peace" (Ps. 37:35-37).

*Chapter 8*

# A PASSION FOR SOULS

ONE OF THE VERY FIRST EVIDENCES of a genuine conversion is the desire that others may share with us in "so great salvation." We often hear that referred to as a "passion for souls," and it is just that. Some Christians seem to retain it only for a little while after their own conversion. In the case of a few, it seems to get stronger as they grow older in the faith. But most of us need to have this holy fire kindled afresh in us from time to time. Let us pray that the Holy Spirit who inspired the chapter now before us may use it to stir us all to greater zeal in the matter of seeking the salvation and eternal welfare of others.

In the previous chapter we heard Queen Esther pleading for her own life, as well as for the lives of her people. Thus we see that she was concerned with something more than her own personal safety. In that respect she was quite different from the Philippian jailer who thought only of himself when he realized what it meant to have to face the God who could shake the prison walls. With no thought, apparently, of his family he simply cried out, "What must I do to be saved?" The apostle not only answered that question, but gave him promise of more when he said, "Believe on the Lord Jesus Christ, and thou shalt be saved, and thy house" (Acts 16:31).

Such is the grace of Him who is "able to do exceeding abundantly above all that we ask or think" (Eph. 3:20).

So far as Esther herself was concerned, we may be sure that her own deliverance was assured when the king ordered the execution of Haman. But nothing was said about her people. She might have thought that their safety was implied. But she was taking nothing for granted. Nor was she the less concerned about them even though she knew that she herself was safe. In that she could put a good many of us to shame. How many there are who never give a moment's thought to the salvation of others! They seem to be quite content with the fact that they themselves have been saved. Like the Philippian jailer to whom we have referred they seem to be occupied only with their own interests. But in this regard Esther was like Rahab of other days who made the two spies who came to Jericho swear unto her by the Lord that they would also show kindness unto her father's house, and that they would save alive her father, her mother, her brothers, and her sisters, and that they would deliver their lives from death (Josh. 2:12, 13). In like manner we now see Esther planning for the salvation, or deliverance, of her people.

"On that day did the king Ahasuerus give the house of Haman the Jews' enemy unto Esther the queen." No doubt this is put at the beginning of this chapter to show us that if Esther had been thinking only of herself she had every reason to be satisfied. It was not so long before this that Haman had "called for his friends, and Zeresh his wife. And Haman told them of the glory of his riches, and the multitude of his children" (Esther 5:10, 11). Now all of this was committed unto Esther to do with as she pleased. In effect, it meant that all the members of that household were really her servants from that day forward. As another illustration of this we may cite the case of Mephibosheth to whom King David gave "all that pertained to Saul and to his house." That that included the servants is shown by the fact that Ziba and his sons were to till the land for Mephibosheth and to bring in the fruits thereof in order that Mephibosheth might lack nothing. And the Scripture is careful to note that "Ziba had fifteen sons and twenty servants" (II Sam. 9:9, 10). We know from Esther 9 that Haman had ten sons, all of which were slain not long after this. It was no small thing, therefore, when the king turned over the house of Haman to Queen Esther.

But even though all was now in her hands, we find that Esther decides to put everything into the hands of Mordecai. And so "Mordecai came before the king; for Esther had told what he was unto her." Not only had the plot of Haman compelled Esther to reveal her identity, but now she also manifests her identification with the very one whom Haman had plotted to hang on the gallows. Such are some of the blessed fruits of persecution! When the people of God are at ease, they tend to drift apart quite easily. It is in times of persecution that they come to value each other, and that by which the enemy hopes to scatter them only serves, under God, to draw them closer together. That is why men like the apostle Paul could actually glory in tribulation. And thus that which we are apt to call a calamity becomes a blessing.

Without a moment's hesitation "the king took off his ring, which he had taken from Haman, and gave it unto Mordecai." It was a sad day for the Jews when Ahasuerus gave that same ring to Haman (Esther 3:10). The document which authorized the extermination of the Jews was sealed with that very ring. The surrender of it was probably the last thing which Haman did in the presence of the king. We have no record of that, of course, but it is implied in verse 2 of our present chapter. And the conferring of that ring upon Mordecai seems to have been the signal for Esther to "set Mordecai over the house of Haman."

Just what Esther's object was in giving this power to Mordecai is not indicated here. But it points to a very beautiful lesson all the same. Vengeance must be taken. But she committed that unto the hands of another. And that is exactly what the word of God exhorts us to do. It is written, "Vengeance is mine; I will repay, saith the Lord" (Rom. 12:19). Long before the Christian era, in referring to the enemies of His people, the Lord said, "To me belongeth vengeance, and recompense; their foot shall slide in due time: for the day of their calamity is at hand, and the things that shall come upon them make haste. For the Lord shall judge his people, and repent himself for his servants, when he seeth that their power is gone, and there is none shut up, or left" (Deut. 32:35, 36). It may be that Queen Esther had those very verses in mind when she turned over the house of Haman to Mordecai.

But to dispose of the house of Haman is one thing, and to provide for the deliverance of her people is another. And so she "spake yet again before the king, and fell down at his feet, and besought him with tears to put away the mischief of Haman the Agagite, and his device that he had devised against the Jews." Haman was no more, but the evil he had done lived on after him. There is a sense in which Satan also has been judged and cast out. In anticipation of His glorious victory over Satan, our Lord could say, "Now is the judgment of this world: now shall the prince of this world be cast out" (John 12:31). But it requires no argument to prove that the evil of which he is the author is still with us. Souls are in jeopardy every moment because of it. And it might well move us to tears as we think of all that is involved in this. We do not read that Esther shed any tears when she pled for her own life. Of course, it is entirely possible that she did not realize at that time all that she had been saved from. And is that not the case with us also?

How many of us realized at the time of our conversion all that the Lord has done for us? But as time goes on, and as we grow in grace and in the knowledge of our Lord and Saviour, we get better acquainted with Him and His Word. In the process we also learn something of the awful predicament that was ours when we were in our sins and under the wrath of God. And when we reflect on the fact that all of the unsaved are still there, we are moved to go forth to snatch them as brands from the burning. It is just as certain as anything could be that if the unsaved were conscious of their present peril, many of them would lose no time in coming to the Saviour. And if we as Christians realized this as we should, there would be more genuine weeping over lost souls, even as the Lord Jesus wept over the city of Jerusalem (Luke 19:41).

It was such earnestness on the part of Queen Esther that caused the king to hold out the golden scepter toward her. "So Esther arose, and stood before the king." Encouraged by this gesture of grace on his part, she rose from her knees to speak to him on behalf of her people. And it is quite remarkable that in her plea there is no reference whatever to the house of Haman. It is the safety of her people that is paramount here. The punishment of the house of Haman will be considered later. So she said, "If it please the king, and if I have found favor in his sight, and the thing seem right before the king, and I be pleasing in his eyes, let it be written to reverse the letters devised by Haman the son of Hammedatha the Agagite, which he wrote to destroy the Jews which are in all the king's provinces." She did not ask him to do something which he did not care to do, or anything that it would not be right to do. She was very careful to consider both his pleasure and his honor. Would that we were always as careful as that when we come to the King of kings with our petitions!

Of course, she did not hide the fact that her own feelings entered into this also. She showed how deeply moved she was when she said, "How can I endure to see the evil that shall come unto my people? or how can I endure to see the destruction of my kindred?" She imagines what it would be like if the mischief of Haman were not put away. She could not bear the thought of it, much less the sight of it. And as I write these words, I wonder how much we are affected by what we know of the future destiny of the lost! The secret of Esther's feelings was bound up in her love for her people and her kindred. Oh, that we loved men enough to weep over them and to plead for them at the throne of Him who is not willing that any should perish but that all should come to repentance!

In his reply to the eloquent plea of Esther, Ahasuerus reminded her and Mordecai that he had already given the house of Haman to Esther, and that Haman had been hanged on the gallows "because he laid his hand upon the Jews." Strictly speaking, this last could hardly have been the immediate reason why Haman was hanged. It was the fact that Harbonah mentioned the gallows upon which Haman intended to hang Mordecai that suggested the verdict, "hang him thereon." Apart from that it would seem that the immediate reason for the execution of Haman was the fact that the king found him "fallen upon the bed whereon Esther was." Here, however, the king made it appear that it was because Haman had laid his hand upon the Jews.

At this point it is very interesting to compare what Ahasuerus said to Esther and Mordecai with what he said to Haman when he gave him permission to write the document of destruction. To Haman he said, "The silver is given thee, the people also, to do with them as it seemeth good unto thee." But to Esther and Mordecai he said, "Write ye also for the Jews, as it liketh you, in the king's name, and seal it with the king's ring: for the writing which is written in the king's name, and sealed with the king's ring, may no man reverse." We note an emphasis here that we do not find in his word to Haman. Can it be that this time he would make it very emphatic that his own heart was in this matter? He surely did not realize when he gave permission to Haman to write as he did, that before long he would be giving permission to others to write that which would annul all that Haman had written. In that sense the king did reverse himself. Nevertheless, this much seems to be clear; he does not expect ever to have to do anything to reverse what Esther and Mordecai are about to do. The previous order was supposedly irrevocable. But it was only the word of a man, after all.

We who trust in the living God have something far better than that. "Men verily swear by the greater: and an oath for confirmation is to them an end of all strife. Wherein God, willing more abundantly to show unto the heirs of promise the immutability of his counsel, confirmed it by an oath: that by two immutable things, in which it was impossible for God to lie, we might have strong consolation, who have fled for refuge to lay hold upon the hope set before us: which hope we have as an anchor of the soul, both sure and steadfast" (Heb. 6:16-19). Esther and Mordecai had two things—the king's name and the king's ring. But we have two better things— God's Word and God's oath.

> How firm a foundation, ye saints of the Lord,
>   Is laid for your faith in His excellent word!
> What more can He say, than to you He hath said,—
>   To you, who for refuge to Jesus have fled?

"Then were the king's scribes called at that time in the third month, that is, the month Sivan, on the three and twentieth day thereof." This third month was the third month of the Jewish *sacred* year, extending from the new moon of our month of May to the new moon of the month of June. This must not be confused with the third month of the Jewish civil year which corresponds roughly to the latter part of November and the first part of the month of December. The third month of the sacred year was the month in which the Jews celebrated the Feast of Weeks, otherwise known as Pentecost. According to Deuteronomy 16:9-12 the Israelite was to number "seven weeks from such time as thou beginnest to put the sickle to the corn. And thou shalt keep the feast of weeks unto the Lord thy God with a tribute of a freewill offering of thine hand, which thou shalt give unto the Lord thy God, according as the Lord thy God hath blessed thee: and thou shalt rejoice before the Lord thy God . . . and thou shalt remember that thou wast a bondman in Egypt."

In Leviticus 23:16 this same time is referred to as "fifty days" at the close of which they were to offer "a new meat [or, meal] offering unto the Lord." In view of what happened at Pentecost after the Lord Jesus ascended to Heaven, it is not difficult to see something of prophetic significance in this. We recall that Mordecai had said that if Esther were to keep silent at that time "then shall enlargement and deliverance arise to the Jews from another place."

We may be sure that in saying that he spoke better than he knew. And while it is true that Esther did not hold her peace, it is also true that deliverance did not come from her, it came from another place. It came from Heaven. It certainly did not come from any earthly source. And it came at the time set by Him who has put the times and the seasons in His own power (Acts 1:7).

Apparently, the wording of the new decree was left entirely to Mordecai for "it was written according to all that Mordecai commanded unto the Jews, and to the lieutenants, and the deputies and rulers of the provinces which are from India unto Ethiopia, an hundred twenty and seven provinces, unto every province according to the writing thereof, and unto every people after their language, and to the Jews according to their writing, and according to their language." It was to be no secret that the Jews were to have the right to defend themselves.

While not exactly like the good news of the Gospel, it was good news in the sense that it offered hope where before there seemed to be no hope. And the fact that it was to be published just as extensively as the bad news had been published is also suggestive of the Gospel. "The soul that sinneth, it shall die" is universal in its scope because all have sinned and come short of the glory of God. But the good news of the Gospel is also universal in its scope "for God so loved the world, that he gave his only begotten Son, that whosoever believeth in him, should not perish, but have everlasting life" (John 3:16).

The decree sent out by Mordecai gave the Jews the right to defend themselves against their enemies. The Christian also has the right to defend himself in his conflict with the Devil and his hosts. Unlike the Jews of Esther's day, "we wrestle not against flesh and blood, but against principalities, against powers, against the rulers of the darkness of this world, against spiritual wickedness [or, wicked spirits] in high places." These are the hosts of Satan who is the prince of the power of the air. Every Christian must be aware of this opposition at times even though he may not always be able to identify it. Of course, Satan may use human instruments to accomplish his ends. No doubt that was the case in Esther's day. Behind Haman and his house was Satan whose desire it has been from the very beginning to destroy the children of God. The murder of Abel marks the beginning of the bloody trail, the culmination of which is seen in the crucifixion of our blessed Lord. And every martyr who has sealed his testimony with his blood is in this noble succession.

But Satan is wise enough to know that "the blood of the martyrs is the seed of the church." Therefore, he prefers at times to wage a "cold war" and thus to wear out the saints of the Most High. It is for that reason that we are exhorted to take unto ourselves the whole armor of God so that we may be able to stand in the evil day; having our loins girt about with truth, and having on the breastplate of righteousness, our feet shod with the preparation of the Gospel of peace; and above all taking the shield of faith wherewith we shall be able to quench all the fiery darts of the wicked one. For our peace of mind we are to have our head covered with the helmet of salvation. But for offensive warfare we are to take the sword of the Spirit, which is the word of God: praying with all prayer and supplication in the Spirit (see Eph. 6:10-18).

Such protection is provided not only for a few of the children of God, but for all of them if they will avail

themselves of it. Our chapter furnishes us with a good illustration of that. We read that Mordecai "wrote in the
king Ahasuerus' name, and sealed it with the king's
ring, and sent letters by posts on horseback, and riders
on mules, camels, and young dromedaries: wherein the
king granted the Jews which were *in every city* to gather
themselves together, and to stand for their life, to destroy,
to slay, and to cause to perish, all the power of the people
and province that would assault them, both little ones and
women, and to take a spoil of them for a prey." If we
look upon "the power of the people" as a type of Satan
which is arrayed against us, we shall have no difficulty
in making the application.

The Jews were to do two things; they were to *gather
together,* and they were to *stand.* In other words, they
were to present a united front against their common foe.
It does not take much imagination to see in this an exact
parallel of what we do when we gather together as the
Lord's people in the place of prayer. It is then that we
actually come into combat with the hosts of wickedness to
which we have already referred. But it is to be feared that
many of God's children know little or nothing about such
warfare. Such conflict requires spiritual energy which is
derived from feeding on the Word of God. Then when
we gather together in the place of prayer, we shall also
be able to stand. And the glorious result will be victories
of faith "in the Lord and in the power of his might."

We note that this chapter makes mention of "spoil."
Paul tells us, by the Spirit, that our Lord Jesus "spoiled
principalities and powers" when He "made a show of
them openly, triumphing over them" (Col. 2:15). We believe that this refers to our Lord's victory over death, and
over him who had the might of death, that is, the Devil.
Our Lord was victorious over death when He rose from

the dead. But His triumph is seen in His ascension to
Heaven, for it was then that He went right through the
domain of Satan who is the prince of the power of the
air. And thus He opened the way for us to come boldly
unto the throne of grace so that we also may triumph in
His triumphs. Because He poured out His soul unto death
it was promised Him that He shall divide the spoil with
the strong (see Isa. 53:12).

There is still another detail in our chapter which reminds us of Ephesians 6 and that is the reference to the
*day:* "Upon *one day* in all of the provinces of king Ahasuerus, namely, upon the thirteenth *day* of the twelfth
month, which is the month Adar. The copy of the writing
for a commandment to be given in every province was
published unto all people, and that the Jews should be
ready against *that day* to avenge themselves on their enemies." In like manner Christians are told to take to themselves the whole armor of God that they may be "able to
withstand in *the evil day*." We have seen already that in
the case of the Jews that day was determined by lot. In
spite of all of his sagacity, the enemy is quite supersti-
tious. But over all of this is the One who has put the
times and the seasons in His own power. And He knows
how to deliver the godly out of his trials and from the
snare of the enemy. Therefore, no day which the enemy
may set for our destruction need take us by surprise.

"So the posts that rode upon mules and camels went
out, being hastened and pressed on by the king's commandment. And the decree was given at Shushan the
palace." There was no time to be lost. No doubt many
a soul is lost, not for lack of information, but because
of procrastination. If the enemy can get us to put off
prayer or anything else which might result in victory
for us, he knows that he can defeat us. It was not only

an exhortation that was sent out that day. It was something more than permission to defend themselves which was granted to the Jews; it was a commandment—yea, "the king's commandment." And what if some "post" or messenger, directed to go to some remote province, had chosen to delay until *the day* had passed! The consequences would have been serious indeed. We, too, have been sent forth with an urgent message. We also live in an evil day. Let us then be on our way and see to it that the place to which we have been sent with the King's commandment shall hear the message of His grace before it be forever too late.

The very fact that this message was "given at Shushan the palace" gave it a royal dignity and importance which brought honor to those chosen to deliver it. Those "posts" were really the king's ambassadors. They were in the king's business. And the content of their message should have made them even more eager to deliver it. Then, too, such a message was bound to find a ready reception on the part of those directly concerned, not only because of the opportunity which it afforded them to defend themselves, but also because royal authority guaranteed the reliability of every word of it. And the same applies to the Gospel as we preach it now. The messenger of the Good News may well consider himself a royal ambassador. And those to whom the message is addressed can rely upon it because it is backed up by all of the power and authority of the King of kings and Lord of lords. In the preamble of the Great Commission our Lord Jesus said, "All power is given unto me in heaven and in earth. Go ye therefore" (Matt. 28:18, 19).

It is in perfect keeping with all of this that we now see Mordecai going out "from the presence of the king in royal apparel of blue and white, and with a great

crown of gold, and with a garment of fine linen and purple." "A dress of blue and white was held in great esti-
mation among the Persians: so that Mordecai, whom the
king delighted to honor, was in fact arrayed in the
royal dress and insignia. The variety and the kind of
insignia worn by a favorite at once makes known to the
people the particular dignity to which he has been raised"
(*Jamieson, Fausset and Brown*). But long before the Persian era the Lord had said, "Speak unto the children of
Israel, and bid them that they make them fringes in the
borders of their garments throughout their generations,
and that they put upon the fringe of the borders a rib-
band of blue: and it shall be unto you for a fringe, that
ye may look upon it, and remember all the commandments of the Lord and do them; and that ye seek not
after your own heart and your own eyes" (Num. 15:38,
39). Thus we can see that *blue* would also have a spiritual
significance for the intelligent Israelite.

It is interesting to observe that there are two different
words used for *crown* in the original language of the
Book of Esther. The one here used differs from that used
to describe the crown worn by Queen Vashti, and later
by Queen Esther. The word here used in the Hebrew is
the same as that of which we have the verb form in
Psalm 8:5, in which we get a preview of our blessed
Lord crowned with glory and honor. "The garment of
fine linen and purple" seems to have been an outer garment worn over another. The fine linen, as we know from
Revelation 19:8, is symbolic of righteousness, and purple
is the well-known symbol of royalty. When we put all
of these things together, we can see that it was no mean
distinction which was conferred upon Mordecai at that
time. It certainly excelled that with which Haman was

compelled to array him as we have seen in our study of chapter 6.

It is quite evident that all of this met with the popular approval. "The city of Shushan rejoiced and was glad." It was not so long before this that that same city "was perplexed" (Esther 3:15). And we may be sure also that those whose destiny was most directly involved in the honor bestowed upon their illustrious compatriot would rejoice in a special way. "The Jews had light, and gladness, and joy, and honor." Even before their actual deliverance they could rejoice in it. That is after the manner of faith. It enables one to look into the future with calm and certainty, knowing that what God promises He is able also to perform (Rom. 4:21).

Verse 16 of our present chapter reminds us very much of Psalm 97:10-12 where we read that the Lord "preserveth the souls of his saints; he delivereth them out of the hand of the wicked. *Light* is sown for the righteous, and *gladness* for the upright in heart. *Rejoice* in the Lord, ye righteous; and give thanks at the remembrance of his holiness." The Jews of Esther's day had every occasion to prove the truth of those words. In place of the darkness, the sorrow, the grief, and the dishonor which had been theirs, they could rejoice in the fourfold blessing of the Lord even though they did not make mention of His name.

This blessing was not limited to the city of Shushan. "In every province, and in every city, whithersoever the king's commandment and his decree came, the Jews had joy and gladness, a feast and a good day." The original word for *feast* in this verse occurs more often in the Book of Esther than in any other book of the Old Testament. It is also translated *banquet* in chapters 5, 6, and 7.

It is first used in the Bible to describe the feast which Lot prepared for the angels who visited him (Gen. 19:3). It is also used to describe the great feast which Abraham made "the same day that Isaac was weaned." Since it is not used in Leviticus 23 we conclude that it was not exactly a religious feast. Nevertheless, we shall see later how it did become a national feast even though it was not numbered among the set times described in Leviticus 23.

The effect of all this upon the people of the land was remarkable. "Many of the people of the land became Jews; for the fear of the Jews fell upon them." They became what we would now call proselytes. The motive which impelled them to do this was not exactly of the highest order. One could wish that we might have heard more about the fear of the Lord than about the fear of the Jews. That which is done for fear of man is apt to change from time to time. But that which is done in the fear of God will abide. He changes not. And it is the fear of the Lord, not the fear of man, which is the beginning of wisdom. It is to be hoped that both the Jews, as well as those who became Jews, learned something of the blessing of that before it was all over.

*Chapter 9*

(verses 1-19)


# THE TABLES TURNED

I<small>N USING THE TITLE</small> which we have given to this chapter we are not unmindful of the fact that it might be taken to mean a mere "change of fortune as in gaming." And the occurrence of the word "turned" in the first verse of the chapter appears to confirm that idea. But there is no such thing as "chance" in the plan and purpose of God, even though Haman did cast lots to determine the day on which he hoped to destroy the Jews. We have seen already that the lot is cast into the lap, but the whole disposing thereof is of the Lord (Prov. 16:33). With that in mind we know that what may appear to be a matter of luck, or chance, is really a part of God's divine purpose.

The favorable turn in the affairs of the Jews was preceded by a more significant turn in the life of the most outstanding Jew of that day, Mordecai himself. In our first acquaintance with him we noted that he was probably one of those who did not take advantage of the opportunity given to return to the land of his fathers when the decree permitting that went forth from King Cyrus. Moreover, it will be recalled that he commanded his cousin Esther to hide her identity in that he bade her not to reveal the fact that she was a Jewess. But when the real test came, and he was called upon to give reverence to Haman, he was bold enough to refuse to do that which was forbidden by the law of Moses.

For a while it looked as though he might have to pay for his refusal with his life. But he stood his ground, and in the end he was honored for that. Indeed, the very one to whom he refused to pay homage was compelled to honor him instead. And then, as we have seen just now in our study of chapter 8, he was promoted much higher. But such honor is not something to be enjoyed as a matter of personal advantage. In the portion now before us we see how Mordecai used his high position for the good and blessing of others. And that is as it should be.

The fateful day "when the king's commandment and his decree drew near to be put in execution" arrived. That was the day when "the enemies of the Jews hoped to have power over them." And we may well imagine how excited everybody would be. Twelve long months had rolled by since that date was set, not because it would take all of that time to make preparation, but because Haman had found it difficult to determine "the lucky day." The fact that it was so difficult to fix the day may account for the statement here that they "hoped to have power over" the Jews. Apparently, there was some doubt about the final outcome after all.

The original word for *power* in this verse is the same as that which is translated *rule* in the next sentence. The Psalmist used the same word in Psalm 119:133 when he prayed, "Order my steps in thy word: and let not any iniquity *have dominion* over me." And the answer to that prayer is found in Romans 6:14 where the apostle Paul tells us by the Spirit that "sin shall not have dominion over you: for ye are not under the law, but under grace." Of such things, naturally, the Jews of that day had no knowledge. But we know that the things which happened unto them were written for our learning. And thus we may learn something of the manner in which the Lord did deliver His own from the power and dominion of sin and Satan when "it was turned to the contrary" and "the Jews had rule over them that hated them."

The Jews' first move was to gather "themselves together in their cities throughout all the provinces of the king Ahasuerus, to lay hand on such as sought their hurt." It would appear from this statement that they had had certain cities assigned to them by the king. In gathering in their own cities they would not unnecessarily expose themselves to the assault of the enemy. In other words, they would not provoke hostility by going where they did not belong. In that they showed more common sense than do some of God's children today. Not a few Christians are caught in the toils of sin and Satan because they insist on going where they have no need to go. Then, too, failure to gather together with their brethren in the appointed place is very often the first step on the downward road of backsliding which leads to defeat. The truly happy man is "the man that walketh not in the counsel of the ungodly, nor standeth in the way of sinners, nor sitteth in the seat of the scornful" (Ps. 1:1).

If the enemy should decide to pursue us even in the place of God's choosing, then it is he who exposes himself to danger and defeat. There may be times when we shall have to meet the enemy on his own ground. But by and large we know that it is far safer to meet him where we may be certain of the complete protection of the Almighty. Then it will be true of us as it was of them in that day, "no man could withstand them; for the fear of them fell upon all the people." "Whatsoever is born of God overcometh the world: and this is the victory that overcometh the world, even our faith" (I John 5:4).

It is interesting to observe that they were helped also by the officers of King Ahasuerus, "because the fear of Mordecai fell upon them. For Mordecai was great in the king's house, and his fame went out throughout all the provinces: for this man Mordecai waxed greater and greater." In this respect he reminds us of King David of whom it is also said that he "waxed greater and greater: for the Lord of hosts was with him" (I Chron. 11:9). In view of such statements it might even be possible to consider Mordecai as a type of the Lord Jesus of whom John the Baptist said, "He must increase, but I must decrease" (John 3:30). Evidently Mordecai went on "increasing" to the end of his life. Truly "the path of the just is as the shining light that shineth more and more unto the perfect day" (Prov. 4:18).

Under such powerful leadership the Jews were well off. "Thus the Jews smote all their enemies with the stroke of the sword, and slaughter, and destruction, and did what they would unto those that hated them." No doubt some may wonder how we can make any application of this to the Christian. We Christians war, but we do not war according to the flesh. The weapons of our warfare are not carnal, but mighty through God to the pulling down of strongholds (II Cor. 10:4). And one of those weapons is called "the sword of the Spirit" (Eph. 6:17).

We gather from the context in which we find this reference to the sword of the Spirit that it is a special weapon for a special kind of warfare. Because it is called "the word of God" some are led to suppose that whenever we use the Word of God we are handling a sword. But such is not the case. In the first place, the expression does not refer to the Bible as a whole. A more accurate translation reads, "the saying of God." And that, I take it, refers to some particular text which we may use in our warfare with the host of wicked spirits. This cannot refer to a warfare with human beings because the text says distinctly that we wrestle not against flesh and blood. It is clear from the context that this is a battle with wicked spirits in the heavenly places.

Now if we think of Haman as a type of the Devil, and his sons and servants as types of those hosts which are under the leadership of the Devil, we shall have no difficulty in making an application for our own instruction and encouragement. The fact that "in Shushan the palace the Jews slew and destroyed five hundred men" lends itself well to such an application. Right there at headquarters, so to speak, we find the enemy in considerable force. And it is reasonable to suppose that they must have identified themselves as enemies of the Jews by some attack upon them, because the Jews laid hands only on such as sought their hurt.

Among those slain in the palace we find the ten sons of Haman all of whom are mentioned by name. And since names had real meaning in those days, it is interesting to see what these may mean. Mr. Thomas Newberry has ventured to give the meanings in the margin of that edition of the Bible which is sometimes referred to as *The Englishman's Bible*. There we are told that Parshandatha means "of noble birth"; Dalphon, "strenuous"; Aspatha, "given by the horse"; Poratha, "ornament"; Aridatha, "great birth"; Parmashta, "strongfisted"; Arisai, "like to a lion"; and Vayzatha, "sincere." He offers no meanings for Adalia and Aridai. But if we may accept as correct the meanings given to the others, then it would appear that this was a proud family. Without doubt the ten sons of Haman took the lead in an attempt to carry out the decree of their father. But not one of them lived to carry on the name of his father.

The historian is careful to note that the Jews did not lay their hand on the spoil. In this they showed more self-control than Achan of whom we read in the Book of Joshua. Among the spoils of Jericho he saw a goodly Babylonish garment, two hundred shekels of silver, and a wedge of gold, and he could not resist the temptation to carry them off. But the Jews at Shushan the palace were not interested in material things. There were bigger things at stake than silver and gold. And they did not allow that which was material and secondary to take their eyes off the real objective. Their existence as a people meant more to them just then than temporary riches. And their behavior at that time exhibits a fine sense of values. Would to God that they had always acted that way! And that goes for the rest of us also.

We come now to the report of all this which was made to the king. "On that day the number of those that were slain in Shushan the palace was brought before the king. And the king said unto Esther the queen, The Jews have slain and destroyed five hundred men in Shushan the palace, and the ten sons of Haman; what have they done in the rest of the king's provinces? now what is thy petition? and it shall be granted thee: or what is thy request further? and it shall be done." Apparently, the king expressed no surprise at the large number of anti-Semites which had been slain in his palace that day. The report from the provinces had not yet come in. But it seems not to matter to him whether the number be large or small, he stands ready to grant the queen even more than she had already received from him. And that shows that what he was doing was not being done grudgingly. While it is true that he did not on this occasion add the familiar words, "even to the half of the kingdom it shall be performed," nevertheless, he did say, "it shall be granted," and "it shall be done."

"Then said queen Esther, If it please the king, let it be granted to the Jews which are in Shushan the palace to do tomorrow also according unto this day's decree, and let Haman's ten sons be hanged upon the gallows." In making this request the queen showed that she was aware of the fact that the decree of Ahasuerus had specified that the Jews should be ready against that day, that is, the thirteenth day of the twelfth month. The decree did not go beyond that one day. But she must have known quite well that there were other enemies who had not yet been apprehended. They may have gone into hiding when they saw what took place. But they were not to be trusted. To allow them to live would be to risk future assaults. They must be completely exterminated.

"And the king commanded it so to be done: and the decree was given at Shushan; and they hanged Haman's ten sons." In view of the fact that Haman's sons had already been slain this may appear to contradict the statement made in verse 12. But we know from II Samuel 21:12 that the corpses of those who had been slain were sometimes hanged afterward to expose them to open shame, as it were. For example, "The bones of Saul and the bones of Jonathan his son" were stolen by the men of Jabesh-gilead, "from the street of Beth-shan, where the Philistines had hanged them, when the Philistines had slain Saul in Gilboa." And such was probably the case here. But we may be sure that Queen Esther would never have requested such a thing without great provocation. If we knew all that was involved in the plot of Haman, we should probably find that her request was fully justified, for she was neither a Jezebel nor an Athaliah.

Royal permission having been obtained for another day of vengeance "the Jews that were in Shushan gathered themselves together on the fourteenth day also of the month Adar, and slew three hundred men at Shushan; but on the prey they laid not their hand." We may well imagine what might have happened later if those three hundred men had been permitted to live. Their continued existence would have constituted a constant threat and danger. In that connection it will be recalled that when the Lord commissioned King Saul to "go and utterly destroy the sinners the Amalekites, and fight against them until they be consumed," he and his people spared Agag the king of the Amalekites, "and the best of the sheep, and of the oxen, and of the fatlings, and the lambs, and all that was good, and would not utterly destroy them: but every thing that was vile and refuse, that they destroyed utterly" (I Sam. 15:9 ff.). It was this failure to carry out the commandment of the Lord that led to the rejection of Saul as king of Israel, and he had to learn through bitter experience that "to obey is better than sacrifice, and to hearken than the fat of rams" (v. 22). The Jews of Esther's day made no such mistake even though we do not read a word about the Lord, or His Word, in the whole account of what they did.

If the anti-Semites of Esther's day were Amalekites, as we have reason to believe they were, then it may be that the Jews did remember that the Lord had said to Moses, "Write this for a memorial in a book, and rehearse it in the ears of Joshua: for I will utterly put out the remembrance of Amalek from under heaven" (Exod. 17:14). That the Jews were to be the divine instruments to accomplish this is clear from the words of Moses in Deuteronomy 25:17-19. "Remember what Amalek did unto thee by the way, when ye were come forth out of Egypt; how he met thee by the way, and smote the hindmost of thee, even all that were feeble behind thee, when thou wast faint and weary; and he feared not God. Therefore it shall be, when the Lord thy God hath given thee rest from all thine enemies round about, in the land which the Lord thy God giveth thee for an inheritance to possess it, that thou shalt blot out the remembrance of Amalek from under heaven; thou shalt not forget it." Had they done that after they were settled in the land, Haman and his house would never have been heard of. Their very existence proved that Israel had failed to carry out this commandment of the Lord. Their present plight was the sad fruit of their disobedience. And that may account for the thoroughness with which they went about their destruction now.

"But the other Jews that were in the king's provinces, gathered themselves together, and stood for their lives, and had rest from their enemies, and slew of their foes seventy and five thousand, but they laid not their hands on the prey." The number of casualties in what was really a defensive action, so far as the Jews were concerned, will give some idea of the magnitude of this plot on the part of the enemy to exterminate them. If they had not "gathered themselves together, and stood for their lives," the final outcome would have been defeat instead of victory and "rest from their enemies." We have already seen the importance of gathering and standing—two things which the Church of our day might well take to heart. Nothing weakens like division, and the enemy knows that. Let us not fail then to learn the lesson from this part of God's Word which will enable us to gain glorious victories over our adversary the Devil.

The Jews that were in the king's provinces required but one day to dispose of their enemies. That was "on the thirteenth day of the month Adar; and on the fourteenth day of the same rested they, and made it a day of feasting and gladness." The fact that they rested on the fourteenth day sounds as though they kept that day as a sabbath. If so, it was not a sabbath of sadness but of gladness, a day of feasting. It was the Lord's plan that the sabbath should be a day of refreshing and rest. "Six days shalt thou do thy work, and on the seventh thou shalt rest: that thine ox and thine ass may rest, and the son of thy handmaid, and the stranger, may be refreshed" (Exod. 23:12).

"But the Jews that were at Shushan assembled together on the thirteenth day thereof, and on the fourteenth thereof; and on the fifteenth day of the same they rested, and made it a day of feasting and gladness." And we like to think that it was likewise a day of thanksgiving to Him who had given them this great deliverance. If the fourteenth day was a sabbath, as we have suggested, then this fifteenth day would be the first day of a new week; another "morrow after the sabbath," as it were.

The difference between "the Jews that were in Shushan" and "the Jews of the villages, that dwell in unwalled towns" is interesting because it may serve as an illustration of the fact that some of the children of God seem to realize and enjoy their deliverance from sin and Satan sooner than others. With some, the joy of being set "free from the law of sin and death" (Rom. 8:2) seems to come immediately after their conversion. In the case of others, that joy seems to be delayed until after they have had an experience such as the apostle Paul describes in Romans 7. But when we cry from the heart,

"O wretched man that I am! who shall deliver me from the body of this death?" then comes the answer, "I thank God through Jesus Christ our Lord." The Jews in Persia knew that they had been delivered, but there is no evidence that they knew, or acknowledged, the One who had delivered them.

Nevertheless, they did celebrate. It was "a day of gladness and feasting, and a good day, and of sending portions one to another." This is very similar to another celebration which took place in Jerusalem some years later, in the days of Nehemiah. At that time "all the people wept, when they heard the words of the law." But Nehemiah said to them, "Go your way, eat the fat, and drink the sweet, and send portions unto them for whom nothing is prepared: for this day is holy unto our Lord: neither be ye sorry; for the joy of the Lord is your strength" (Neh. 8:9, 10). This was not quite so spontaneous as the celebration in the days of Esther, but it was much more spiritual. The people of Nehemiah's day knew who it was who had delivered them and had given them occasion to feast.

The Jews of Esther's day apparently took no notice of their divine Host. And many professing Christians of our day are guilty of the same thing. They celebrate Thanksgiving Day, Christmas, and Easter with little or no thought of the One who gives those days their true significance. And to behold non-Christians celebrating those days seems strange indeed. But that goes to show that we who know the true significance of such days should be more careful than ever to preserve it. In so doing we might be used of the Lord to lead others to discover it for themselves. This is a much-needed ministry in this land of ours.

# MEMORIAL DAYS

THE CUSTOM of marking out certain days to commemorate special events dates back to the beginning of history when the Lord set aside the seventh day to celebrate the conclusion of the work of creation. Again, when He delivered His people from Egypt and its bondage He said, "Remember this day, in which ye came out from Egypt, out of the house of bondage; for by strength of hand the Lord brought you out from this place. . . . This day came ye out in the month Abib" (Exod. 13:3, 4). In like manner, those of us who know the Lord Jesus Christ as our personal Saviour also remember with praise and gratitude the day when we first knew the joy of sins forgiven and peace with God. For us too, the first day of the week, that day on which our blessed Lord rose again from the dead, will ever be a most important day. Triumphantly we sing, "The stone which the builders refused is become the head stone of the corner. This is the Lord's doing; it is marvelous in our eyes. This is the day which the Lord hath made; we will rejoice and be glad in it" (Ps. 118:22-24).

The days of which our present portion speaks had never been set aside before. They are not referred to in

Leviticus 23 which gives us a list of all the holy days and seasons which the children of Israel were to celebrate each year. None of them occurred in the month Adar, which is the last month of the sacred year. There was no conflict, therefore, with that which had been prescribed by the law of Moses. And the fact that the Jews still celebrate these days each year indicates that they accept the institution as valid. Of course, there is no divine directive such as we find in Leviticus 23, but the man who took the lead in establishing this custom was none other than Mordecai who ranked, for the time being, with other great leaders of Israel.

It was Mordecai who "wrote these things, and sent letters unto all the Jews that were in all the provinces of the king Ahasuerus, both nigh and far, to establish this among them, that they should keep the fourteenth day of the month Adar, and the fifteenth day of the same, yearly, as the days wherein the Jews rested from their enemies, and the month which was turned unto them from sorrow to joy, and from mourning into a good day: that they should make them days of feasting and joy, and of sending portions one to another, and gifts to the poor" (Esther 9:20-22).

It is to be remarked that nothing is said here about the destruction of their enemies. Instead of that we have the very meaningful expression, "The Jews rested from their enemies." We have but to single it out in this way to see how suggestive it is of that rest which the Lord Jesus gives to all those who come to Him. Says He, "Come unto me, all ye that labor and are heavy laden, and I will give you rest" (Matt. 11:28). If the labor were merely self-ordered labor, one might stop at any time. If the burden were self-imposed, one might drop it at any time. The implication, however, is that the labor is slave toil ordered by a taskmaster as real as any that the children of Israel ever had in the land of Egypt. And the burden with which we were so heavily laden was a burden placed upon our necks by one who would have enslaved us forever. In offering to give us rest from these, the Lord Jesus offered to set us free from the domination of sin and Satan—two of the greatest enemies we have. But our divine Emancipator has removed our sins as far as the East is from the West,

> And rest divine is ours instead,
> Whilst glory crowns His brow.

When Zacharias, the father of John the Baptist, celebrated the birth of the forerunner of our Lord, he made reference to the fact that the Israelites should be saved from their enemies and from the hand of all who hated them, and that being delivered out of the hand of their enemies they might serve the Lord without fear, in holiness and righteousness before Him, all the days of their life (see Luke 1:71-75). It is certain that Zacharias was thinking of the Messiah of Israel who alone could bring such deliverance to His people. And we may be sure that he was also thinking of something more than mere human enemies. A man of his spiritual stature could never be satisfied with political freedom only. True freedom comes from Him of whom it is written, "If the Son shall make you free, ye shall be free indeed" (John 8:36).

The second great thing to be noticed here is that these memorial days occur in "the month which was turned unto them from sorrow to joy, and from mourning into a good day." Once again we are reminded of the words of our Lord Jesus who said, "Verily, verily, I say unto you, That ye shall weep and lament, but the world shall rejoice: and ye shall be sorrowful, but your sorrow shall be turned into joy. . . . Ye now therefore have sorrow: but I will see you again, and your heart shall rejoice, and your joy no man taketh from you" (John 16:20, 22). And we have good reason to believe that it was the same One who turned that month of sorrow into joy in the days of Esther even though the Jews did not recognize Him at the time. Even then it was true that "he was in the world, and the world was made by him, and the world knew him not. He came unto his own, and his own received him not" (John 1:10, 11). We believe that the verses just quoted refer to Old Testament times, and that the great deliverance wrought in the days of Esther and Mordecai was one of those gracious manifestations of the One who was yet to come. He alone can make transformations such as we read of here. "This also cometh forth from the Lord of hosts, which is wonderful in counsel, and excellent in working" (Isa. 28:29).

The third thing which was to characterize this festive occasion was the sending of portions one to another, and the sending of gifts to the poor. How easy it is to observe the first part of this as is so often done at Christmas and Easter, while the second part is quite forgotten! Many a Christmas celebration has become nothing more than "an exchange of gifts," and is actually referred to in that way. To be sure, there is nothing wrong with such a custom. But we must not stop there. The Jews were to send gifts to those from whom they could expect nothing in return. Our Lord said, "If ye do good to them which do good to you, what thank have ye? for sinners also do even the same . . . love ye your enemies, and do good, and lend, hoping for nothing again; and your reward shall be great, and ye shall be the children of the Highest:

for he is kind unto the unthankful and to the evil" (Luke 6:33, 35).

How good it is to read that "the Jews undertook to do as they had begun, and as Mordecai had written unto them; because Haman the son of Hammedatha, the Agagite, the enemy of all the Jews, had devised against the Jews to destroy them, and had cast Pur, that is, the lot, to consume them, and to destroy them"! As I write these words I have before me a news report published in the *Chicago Daily News* for March 18, 1954, concerning the celebration of the Purim festival in the various synagogues of the city. Among the titles of the sermons to be delivered by the different rabbis, I find this one, "Are We Faced with a New Haman?" Just how the rabbi intended to answer that question was not indicated in the article. But the very mention of the name of Haman shows that he is still looked upon as typical of one who may be seeking the destruction of the Jewish people.

Just as the name of Quisling has become the modern epithet for one who undermines his own country from within, and just as the name of Judas Iscariot is always associated with the worst form of treason, so the name of Haman will always stand out as the typical anti-Semite. He is here described as "the enemy of all the Jews." And we must never forget that this anti-Semitism was just a part of a greater scheme to destroy, if possible, "the seed" who was to bruise the serpent's head (Gen. 3:15).

"But when Esther came before the king, he commanded by letters that his wicked device, which he had devised against the Jews, should return upon his own head, and that he and his sons should be hanged on the gallows." The name of *Esther* is not actually in the original text here. The American Standard Version renders it, "When *the matter* came before the king." But the new Revised

Standard Version has restored the name of the queen. The matter would never have come before the king if Esther had not risked her life to bring it to his attention. In the news article referred to above we find the statement that the festival of Purim "recalls the heroism of Esther, who risked her life to aid the Jewish people."

"Wherefore they called these days Purim after the name of Pur," that is, the lot. Haman and his sons meant it for evil, "but God meant it unto good, to bring to pass, as it is this day, to save much people alive" (Gen. 50:20). I have quoted these words of Joseph to his brethren to show that this was not the first time that the Lord brought good out of that which was designed for evil. And that should give every child of God comfort. Our God is able to turn the darkest day into a shining light. There is nothing too hard for Him.

"Therefore for all the words of this letter, and of that which they had seen concerning this matter, and which had come unto them, the Jews ordained, and took upon them, and upon their seed, and upon all such as joined themselves unto them, so as it should not fail, that they would keep these two days according to their writing, and according to their appointed time every year; and that these days should be remembered and kept throughout every generation, every family, every province, and every city; and that these days of Purim should not fail from among the Jews, nor the memorial of them perish from their seed."

It is very interesting to see how they connect the written word with their experience—namely, that which they had seen and that which had come upon them. When experience agrees with the written Word of God, the combination is happy indeed. The Jews who had passed through those dark days confirmed the reasons for the observation of these days of Purim. They not only bound themselves to perpetual observation of these days, but in the undertaking they included also the generations yet to come, as well as any proselytes who might join themselves to them, regardless of where they might be living. In their thinking they included every generation, every family, every province, and every city. Thus we can see that the ecumenicity of which we hear so much nowadays is not such a new idea.

Christians also have a "memorial" which is ecumenical in its meaning and intent. We may not be able to sit down at the same table with every Christian in the world, but when we break bread in remembrance of our blessed Lord, there is a sense in which we are having fellowship with every Christian; for "we being many are one bread, and one body: for we are all partakers of that one bread" (I Cor. 10:17).

The part that Queen Esther played in all of this is also very interesting. In this she stands out in contrast to Ruth, the only other woman who had the honor of having a book of the Bible named after her. In the case of Ruth, we note as we come to the close of the book which bears her name that she becomes less and less prominent. She is passive rather than active. But in the case of Esther we find just the opposite. "Then Esther the queen, the daughter of Abihail, and Mordecai the Jew, wrote with all authority, to confirm this second letter of Purim." This is the second time that Esther is referred to as the daughter of Abihail. When she was first discovered as a possible candidate to take the place of the deposed Vashti, she was referred to as the daughter of Abihail (Esther 2:15). After that, no reference is made to her father until we come to this. Now, instead of trying to conceal her ancestry, the sacred historian seems to emphasize it.

And even though Mordecai is referred to again and again as "the Jew," we never find that to be the case with Esther. Of course, we know that when Mordecai was referred to as "the Jew," it was not always in a complimentary way. Here it is mentioned as if that were the greatest distinction he might claim. He probably had more than one title by this time. But it is not by his titles that he is known here, but by his racial and ancestral connections. That which was once a reproach now becomes the greatest honor.

This is the more remarkable when we take into account that the letter which was being sent out was written "with all authority." It is just here that one might have expected to see some title affixed. But evidently "Mordecai the Jew" was the most dignified thing that could be said of him. And such is the case of a true Christian. The most wonderful thing anyone can say about him is that "he is a Christian." Even the non-Christian recognizes that. All the titles and the degrees which men may confer on such can never surpass, or excel, in dignity and glory the name which completely identifies us with Him who loved us and gave Himself for us.

"And he sent the letters unto all the Jews, to the hundred twenty and seven provinces of the kingdom of Ahasuerus, with words of peace and truth." Over and above the letters which made the observance of the feast mandatory, we find these "words of peace and truth." That indicates that in the writing of this letter, Mordecai was acting as something more than a prime minister giving orders to those under his authority; he was a minister ministering to the spiritual needs of his people as well. This is so Christlike that we cannot resist making the comparison. "The law was given by Moses, but grace and truth came by Jesus Christ" (John 1:17). Thus were these

days of Purim confirmed "in their times appointed, according as Mordecai the Jew and Esther the queen had
enjoined them, and as they had decreed for themselves
and for their seed, the matters of the fastings and their
cry."

The fact that the people themselves had decreed these
things for themselves and their descendants shows that
there was perfect agreement between them and those who
enjoined, or commanded, these things. In that we get a
good illustration of a principle which we believe may be
traced all through the Bible. If one loves the Lord his
God with all his heart and mind and soul, he will not find
it irksome to keep His commandments. And if that were
true of those who were under the law, how much more
should it be true of those of us whose hearts have been
captivated by His love and grace? Obedience then becomes a matter of loving obligation.

And the fact that "their seed," that is, their children,
were included shows that what was right and proper
for the parents was right and proper also for those who
were to come after them. That is quite different, of
course, from that philosophy which teaches that we
should not impose upon our children that which we believe until they are able to decide for themselves whether
or not they desire to be governed accordingly. No one
knows better what is best for his children than one who
has been saved by grace from a life of sin and its terrible
consequences. He may well decree that his "seed" shall
follow after him in these things. It was said of Abraham,
"I know him, that he will command his children and his
household after him, and they shall keep the way of the
Lord, to do justice and judgment; that the Lord may
bring upon Abraham that which he hath spoken of him"
(Gen. 18:19). And that is as it should be with all of us.

And that it results in blessing for all concerned can be proved by scores of cases of Christian parents who have brought up their children in the nurture and admonition of the Lord.

"The matters of the fastings and their cry" take us back, of course, to the dark days when the threat of death hung over their heads. In the joy of their deliverance they could not forget what they had been delivered from. In like manner, the memory of our low estate before the Lord saved us by His grace should serve to make us truly grateful, as well as joyful. Would to God that we all knew more about "the matters of the fastings and their cry"! Perhaps one reason why we do not say more about this is because there was not much fasting and crying to begin with. But wherever there has been deep conviction of sin and true repentance there will be found a corresponding sense of gratitude to the Lord. It will be like the "bitter herbs" that were to be eaten with the Passover lamb. In themselves they were not pleasant to taste, but they served to bring out the flavor of the lamb.

"And the decree of Esther confirmed these matters of Purim; and it was written in the book." Thus a permanent record was made of these matters so that they might be preserved for generations yet to come. And to this day we find that "the book" is still referred to even by those who seem to have no appreciation of its spiritual depth and value. But for those of us who accept the doctrine of the verbal inspiration of the Bible, the fact that it was written in "the book" is significant. And that is one of the best of reasons we have for studying this Book of Esther. The things which are written here were "written for our learning, that we through patience and comfort of the scriptures might have hope" (Rom. 15:4).

*Chapter 10*

# THE GREATNESS OF MORDECAI

IN THIS BRIEF CHAPTER of only three verses we have something more than an appendix to the Book of Esther. Commenting on the opening verse, A. T. Olmstead remarks in his *History of the Persian Empire* that "without a word of protest, the populous and wealthy Greek cities of Asia were surrendered to a monarch whom poets and orators never wearied of describing as *the barbarian*." From that we gather that the laying of "a tribute upon the land, and upon the isles of the sea," was no more popular in those days than a similar tax would be now.

The sea referred to here is probably the Mediterranean. That being so, we can see how far west the Persian Empire may have extended. Some think that the power of Ahasuerus extended beyond the coasts of Greece to Italy and even as far west as Spain. But the eastern and western limits named in the very first verse of this Book of Esther certainly give the actual extent of the empire.

One commentator takes the view that "the isles" mentioned here were islands in the Persian Gulf. But a glance at the map would hardly confirm that view. The few coastal islands shown there do not begin to compare in size and importance with such islands as Cyprus and Crete in the Mediterranean. But even though we may not be able to say with certainty which islands are here

126

referred to, the fact remains that Ahasuerus was evidently in need of funds, and hence the tribute, or tax. According to secular history, he had projected an unsuccessful expedition into Greece, and as a result his treasury was badly depleted. But for all of that his scribes were diligent in recording "all the acts of his power, and of his might . . . in the book of the chronicles of the kings of Media and Persia."

But the things that interest us even more than that statement is "the declaration of the greatness of Mordecai, whereunto the king advanced him . . . for Mordecai the Jew was next unto king Ahasuerus." The word here rendered *declaration* is found but twice in the Old Testament, and both times in this Book of Esther. The other reference is in Esther 4:7 where it is rendered *sum*. And strangely enough, even though it refers there to "the sum of money that Haman had promised to pay to the king's treasuries for the Jews, to destroy them," it was Mordecai who used the word. But here it is used to describe the measure of Mordecai's greatness. There is something ironical about that. It sounds as though the Lord was actually making a mockery of Haman's promise. Now it so happens that the word for *stingeth* in Proverbs 23:32 comes from the same root in the Hebrew. And one can see how the declaration of the greatness of Mordecai would sting those who had sought his ruin. It is another illustration of the turning of the tables, as it were.

But Mordecai was not only great in the court of Ahasuerus, he was also "great among the Jews, and accepted of the multitude of his brethren." And that must have meant a great deal to him. Very often, as the Lord Jesus warns us, a man is not without honor save in his own country and in his own house. Happily, such was not the case here. And to say that he was accepted of the multitude of his brethren means that they were unanimously pleased with him; they were satisfied with him. And they had good reason to be. When we think of his defiance of Haman, we can see how some of them might question his wisdom at times. But no one could question his courage.

The greatness of Mordecai never inflated him. He never became a megalomaniac. On the contrary, he was most altruistic, ever "seeking the wealth of his brethren, and speaking peace to all his seed." Their wealth here must not be understood to refer merely to their material wealth. The word here used for *wealth* means their good in its widest possible sense. We may well suppose that by virtue of his high position and great authority, he would be able to initiate legislation which would promote the well-being of the people. But he was even more than a legislator and administrator, he was a counselor and a preacher, "speaking peace to all his seed."

And so the book closes with a living man active in the best interests of all concerned. The fact that we have no record of his death is quite remarkable, because the history of most men concludes with some sort of obituary. Not so with Mordecai. Thus the impression is left in our minds of one who lives on and on. "He that doeth the will of God abideth forever" (I John 2:17).